GUIDE
VALLEY OF
AND TO THE THEBAN NECF

ALBERTO SILIOTTI

THE AMERICAN UNIVERSITY IN CAIRO PRESS

GUIDE TO THE
VALLEY OF THE KINGS
AND TO THE THEBAN NECROPOLISES AND TEMPLES

Texts and photographs
Alberto Siliotti

Editorial coordination
Laura Accomazzo

Graphic design
Patrizia Balocco Lovisetti

Maps
Oxford Cartographers

Translation by
Hever, Tel Aviv (Israel)
Ann Ghiringhelli

© 1996 White Star S.r.l.
Via C. Sassone, 22/24 - 13100 Vercelli, Italy
www.whitestar.it

Published in Egypt in 2002 by
The American University in Cairo Press
113 Sharia Kasr el Aini, Cairo, Egypt
www.aucpress.com

Dar el Kutub No. 4748/02
ISBN 977 424 718 3

The tombs described in this book were selected by the author following criteria of scientific interest, artistic value, accessibility to the public and space restrictions imposed by the publisher.

1 This little gilded wooden statue of the goddess Selkis was found in the tomb of Tutankhamun (KV no. 62) near the large shrine of gilded wood containing the canopic vases with the king's entrails.
(Cairo Museum)

2-3 The gold mask of Tutankhamun is one of the masterpieces of world art and is undoubtedly the most admired exhibit of the Cairo Museum. The solid gold mask, weighing about ten kilos, was fitted directly over the king's mummy.
(Cairo Museum)

4 Gold amulet of a female-headed winged uraeus discovered on the mummy in the tomb of Tutankhamun (KV no. 62). The uraeus was the sacred cobra, protector of royalty, and it appeared among the numerous amulets arranged on the pharaoh's mortal remains so as to ensure him a magical protection.
(Cairo Museum)

5 In the vestibule of her tomb (QV no. 66), Nefertari Meri-en-Mut, Ramesses II's "Great Royal Bride", whose name means "the Most Beautiful, Beloved of Mut", is introduced to different deities. In the image shown here, from the southern side of the vestibule, the queen is led hand in hand by the falcon-headed god Harsiesis.

PREFACE

The Valley of the Kings and the tombs of the nobles are, together with the pyramids of Giza, the most visited and best-known archaeological sites of all Egypt. They are a never-failing attraction to the tourists coming to visit Luxor – the ancient Thebes – even for a single day. The tombs of Thebes are among the masterpieces of world art for the quality of their pictorial decorations, so much so that UNESCO has classified them as "World Heritage" sites. However, unlike the Giza pyramids, the tombs are extremely heterogeneous and their topography is complex and hardly understandable for the hasty tourist who finds himself being literally "carried" from one monument and from one tomb to the other, often receiving fanciful or very scanty explanations.

Incredibly, despite the very high number of visitors, a complete guide to the Theban necropolis has never been published. Now, this gap is being filled by this "Guide to the Valley of the Kings and to the Theban Necropolises and Temples" that presents for the first time the whole archaeological area under consideration, making use of topographical maps and reliefs prepared especially for this work, and setting out updated and scientifically

accurate data, previously hidden in obscure specialized journals, utterly out of the reach of a non-Egyptologist. For the first time, each tomb is described in a concise, yet detailed manner, with a plan on which the most important or interesting mural paintings are located and shown. The Theban temples are also explained point by point in their architectural structures and decorations, with the assistance of numerous topographical plans. The guide is completed by suggested walking itineraries in the Theban mountain, with a map of routes which allow the visitor not only to see Thebes's monuments from unusual points of view, but also to explore new and surprising spots: prehistorical sites, rocky temples, graffiti of the pharaonic era, huts and villages where the ancient craftsmen used to live, and rock quarries from which the colors used for the decoration of the tombs were extracted. A glossary setting out technical terms and names of divinities, concisely presented for the purpose of rendering the text more "reader-friendly", closes this unique guide – the fruit of five years of work and field surveys.

7 bottom left This photograph shows the Deir el-Bahri site with the temple of Hatshepsut and, on the left, the temples of Tuthmosis III and Nebhepetre Mentuhotep.

7 bottom right The first pylon of Ramesses III's great memorial temple at Medinet Habu. On the left there is the chapel of the Divine Adoratrices of Amun, who enjoyed a very great power and prestige in the age of the Twenty-Fifth and Twenty-Sixth Dynasties. The temple of Ramesses III is the best preserved among all the royal cult temples built on the western bank of the Nile.

INTRODUCTION

Thebes, the great capital of Egypt during the New Kingdom, was a crowded city stretching along the Nile's eastern bank, in the area extending between the present little town of Luxor and its suburb Karnak, about 500 kilometers south of Cairo. The ancient Egyptians called the city *Waset*, "the City of the Scepter", capital of Egypt's Fourth Nome. It was the Greeks, many centuries later, who called it Thebes, a name already used by Homer who speaks of "Thebes of the Hundred Gates", referring not so much to the city's "gates" but to the impressive pillars of *Ipet-isut* "the Most Privileged of Seats", as the nearby temple of Karnak, Egypt's largest temple built to the glory of Amun "the Unknowable, the King of Gods", was called. Thebes, the city of the living built on the Nile's eastern bank, was the kingdom of Amun, whose earthly son was the pharaoh. On the opposite bank of the Nile, at the foot of the Theban mountain – the sacred mountain – where the sun sets, stretched the capital's huge royal and civilian necropolis: this was the kingdom of Osiris, "Lord of the Afterlife", called by the Egyptians *imentit en waset*, "the West of Thebes", or *Ta Geser* "the Sacred Land". The west bank did not include only the tombs of the kings of Egypt, of their families and of the leading dignitaries, the paintings in which are among the greatest art of all time. It was also the place where the worship of the deified living king, besides that of the dead kings, was conducted in the so-called "temples of millions of years" – masterpieces of ancient architecture. The royal necropolises, referred to as the "Valley of the Kings" and the "Valley of the Queens", the private necropolises – the "tombs of the nobles"– and the great memorial temples, such as Deir el-Bahri, the Ramesseum and Medinet Habu, have nowadays become tourist attractions visited every year by millions who wish to admire the works of art enclosed in the ancient kingdom of Osiris.

OLD KINGDOM 2658-2150 BC
FIRST INTERMEDIATE PERIOD
2150-2100 BC
MIDDLE KINGDOM 2100-1750 BC
SECOND INTERMEDIATE PERIOD
1750-1550 BC

NEW KINGDOM 1550-1076 BC
Eighteenth Dynasty 1550-1295 BC

Ahmosis	1550-1525
Amenophis I	1525-1504
Thutmosis I	1504-1492
Thutmosis II	1492-1479
Hatshepsut	1479-1457
Thutmosis III	1479-1425
Amenophis II	1427-1397
Thutmosis IV	1397-1387
Amenophis III	1387-1349
Amenophis IV / Akhenaten	1349-1333
Smenkhkare	1335-1333
Tutankhamun	1333-1324
Ay	1324-1321
Horemheb	1321-1295

Nineteenth Dynasty 1295-1188 BC

Ramesses I	1295-1294
Sethos I	1294-1279
Ramesses II	1279-1213
Merneptah	1213-1204
Amenemesses	1204-1201
Sethos II	1201-1195
Siptah	1195-1190
Twosret	1190-1188

Twentieth Dynasty 1188-1076 BC

Setenakhte	1188-1186
Ramesses III	1186-1154
Ramesses IV	1154-1148
Ramesses V	1148-1144
Ramesses VI	1144-1136
Ramesses VII	1136-1128
Ramesses VIII	1128-1125
Ramesses IX	1125-1107
Ramesses X	1107-1098
Ramesses XI	1098-1076

THIRD INTERMEDIATE PERIOD
1076-712 BC
LATE PERIOD 712-332 BC
GRECO-ROMAN PERIOD
332 BC - 395 AD

8 left The emblem of the Fourth Nome, called waset, *"the Scepter", which included the Theban area, was at the same time Thebes's old toponym. The nomes were Egypt's administrative subdivisions. During the New Kingdom, there were 42 of them.*

8 center Amun was the main deity in the Theban pantheon. Together with his spouse Mut and his son Khonsu, they formed the so-called "Theban Triad". Amun, a name that means "the Unknowable", was the king of the gods and used to be represented in human shape with his head decorated with two tall plumes, while his flesh was painted in blue – color of the air and of the sky. (Ippolito Rosellini, Monumenti Storici)

8-9 The tomb of Ramose (TT no. 55) in the necropolis of Sheikh Abd el-Qurna is decorated with bas-reliefs of supreme stylistic perfection – like these, showing guests attending the funeral banquet. Ramose was a very high-ranking dignitary who bore the title of "Governor of the Town and Vizier" and lived in the time of Amenophis IV.

WESTERN THEBES

Western Valley

WV no. 22
Amenophis III

WV no. 23
Ay

KV no. 62
Tutankhamun

Valley of the
Kings

Deir
el-Bahri

Temple of
Hatshepsut

Temple of
Mentuhotep

▲ El-Qurn

Sheikh Abd
el-Qurna

Upper
Enclosure

L
En

Deir
el-Medina

Ptolemaic
Temple

Rame

Valley of the
Queens

Temple c
Tuthmosis

Temple of
Merneptah

Medinet Habu

Temple of
Ramesses III

E.A.O. Office
(Egyptian
Antiquities
Organization)

Temple
Amenop

Malqatta Royal
Palace of
Amenophis III

Temple of the
Tuthmosids

Colossi
Memn

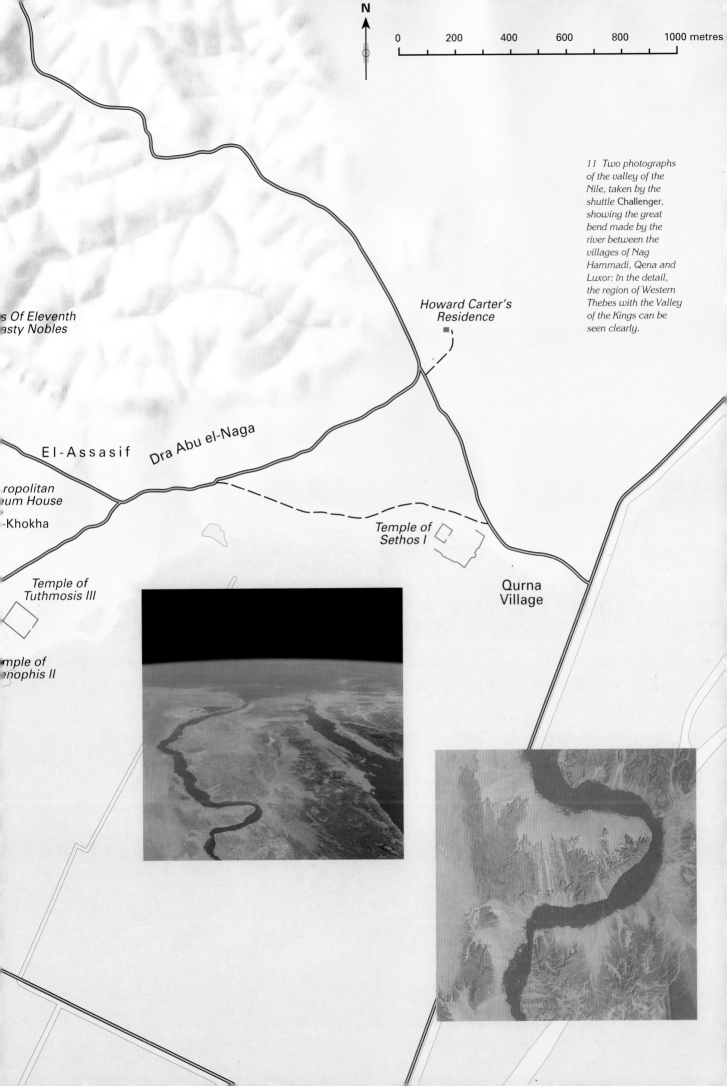

N

0 200 400 600 800 1000 metres

s Of Eleventh
asty Nobles

Howard Carter's
Residence

El-Assasif   Dra Abu el-Naga

ropolitan
eum House

-Khokha

Temple of
Sethos I

Temple of
Tuthmosis III

Qurna
Village

mple of
enophis II

11 Two photographs
of the valley of the
Nile, taken by the
shuttle Challenger,
showing the great
bend made by the
river between the
villages of Nag
Hammadi, Qena and
Luxor: in the detail,
the region of Western
Thebes with the Valley
of the Kings can be
seen clearly.

THE ROYAL NECROPOLISES
THE VALLEY OF THE KINGS

12-13 The Valley of the Kings, the name by which Champollion first called this site, was the royal necropolis of the Theban pharaohs of the New Kingdom. The Egyptians in fact called this site by the official name "the Great and Majestic Necropolis of the Millions of Years of the Pharaoh, Life, Strength, Health in the West of Thebes", or more simply as Ta-sekhet-aat – "Great Field".

The Valley of the Kings is a deep wadi, hollowed in the rocks of the Theban mountain, which splits into two arms: the main one forms the Valley of the Kings proper; the other is the Western Valley where only four tombs are found, among which are those of the pharaohs Ay (WV no. 23), Tutankhamun's successor, and Amenophis III (WV no. 22).

The Valley of the Kings, called by the Arabs *Biban el-Muluk* (that is "the Gates of the Kings") because of the entrances of several tombs opening in the valley's rocky walls, is dug out of the limestones of the Libyan range and directed mainly southwest–northeast.

The ancient Egyptians referred to it in different ways, such as *Ta-sekhet-aat* – "Great Field" – or "the Beautiful Ladder of the West", but its official name was "the Great and Majestic Necropolis of the Millions of Years of the Pharaoh, Life Strength Health in the West of Thebes".

Today the access to the valley, several kilometers long, is over a wide asphalted road that follows the ancient track used in the pharaonic era and referred to as the "Road where Re Sets". The valley is divided into two branches: the western one is called the Western Valley, and also the Valley of the Monkeys, and it shelters four tombs, two of which are royal and belong to the pharaohs

12 bottom Mount El-Qurn, also called the "Theban Peak" owing to its shape reminiscent of a pyramid, dominates the Theban necropolis and the Valley of the Kings. The presence of this natural element, so highly evocative, was probably one of the reasons that contributed to the choice of the Valley of the Kings as a royal necropolis.

Amenophis III (WV no. 22) and Ay (WV no. 23), while the main branch, which is found on the extension of the access road, is the one commonly referred to as the Valley of the Kings and encloses 58 tombs.

The Valley of the Kings is dominated by the Theban Peak, called by the natives el-Qurna, "the Horn", from its curious pyramid-like shape, identified in ancient times with the cobra-goddess Mertseger, "She Who Loves Silence". It was probably the presence of such a geomorphological element, clearly calling to mind the pyramid, a peculiarity of the Old Kingdom's royal burials, that prompted the first pharaohs of the Eighteenth Dynasty to single out this imposing spot, burned by the desert sun, for the establishment of their eternal dwellings. To this religious and ritual motive a more practical one is certainly to be added: as a result of its position and its geographical conformation, the access to this valley was difficult and could easily be supervised by the *Medjay*, the special police corps entrusted with the guarding of the necropolises.

It is hard to ascertain who was the first pharaoh who had himself buried in the valley, although Tuthmosis I, occupying KV no. 38, seems to be entitled to the priority. This tomb, however, may have been arranged later, at the time of Tuthmosis III, who may have transferred there the sarcophagus of the first of the Tuthmosids, as is indicated by the objects found in it, which go back to the times of Tuthmosis III.

One of the most ancient tombs, if not the most ancient, is certainly the gigantic and unusual one intended by Hatshepsut for herself and her father, Tuthmosis I (KV no. 20). However, the possibility cannot be ruled out that the hypogeum was originally indeed built for Tuthmosis I and that Hatshepsut had extended the original plan.

13 top The cobra-goddess Mertseger, "She Who Loves the Silence", was thought of as the incarnation of Mount El-Qurn, the Theban mountain, and was generally represented in the shape of a cobra-headed woman, occasionally adorned with a Hathoric crown. Mertseger exercised a protective function over the necropolises and over the dead.

13 bottom Pharaoh Tuthmosis I (Queen Hatshepsut's father and the successor of Amenophis I), who reigned between 1504 and 1492 BC, was probably the first pharaoh to be buried in the Valley of the Kings, but the exact circumstances of his burial and which tomb was his original one still remain a mystery.

THE VALLEY OF THE KINGS

14-15 In the Valley of the Kings there are sixty-two known tombs, only twenty-four among them being royal burials. To the right the ancient paths travelled by the craftsmen working on the construction of the tombs and dwelling in the nearby town of Deir el-Medina and the so-called "village of the hill", a small inhabited area with dried walls where, in times of hard work, the workmen lived temporarily.

KV no. 8
Merneptah

KV n.
Rames

KV no. 9
Ramesses VI/V

KV no.
Tutankh

KV no. 12

KV no. 57
Horemheb

KV no. 58

KV no. 56

KV no. 35
Amenophis II

KV no. 49-52

KV no. 53

KV no. 11
Ramesses III

KV no.
Amenemes

KV no. 36

KV no. 61

KV no. 29

KV no. 13

KV no.14
Sethenakhte/
Twosret

KV no. 47
Siptah

KV no. 40

KV no. 38
Tuthmosis I

KV no. 26

KV no. 30

KV no. 15
Sethos II

KV no. 59

KV no. 31

KV no. 32

KV no. 37

KV no. 42

KV no. 33

KV no. 34
Tuthmosis III

KV no. 2
Ramesses IV

Luxor

Toward KV no. 1 (Tomb of
Ramesses VII), Western
Valley, Car Parking

KV no. 3

KV no. 46

KV no. 4
Ramesses XI

KV no. 5

KV no. 6
Ramesses IX

o. 55

KV no. 45

KV no. 44

KV no. 16
Ramesses I

KV no. 28

KV no. 27

no. 17
hos I

KV no. 18
Ramesses X

KV no. 54

KV no. 21

Path to
Deir el-Bahri

KV no. 60

KV no. 20
Hatshepsut

KV no. 19
Montu-her-khepshef

KV no. 43
Tuthmosis IV

N

0   20   40   60   80   100 metres

In any case, starting from the times of Hatshepsut and Tuthmosis III, the Valley of the Kings became the Theban pharaohs' burial place and continued serving as a royal necropolis until the end of the Twentieth Dynasty, specifically until the time of Ramesses XI, who was the last pharaoh buried in the Valley. Contrary to popular belief, the entrances to the royal tombs were not hidden but clearly visible, and the necropolis police, besides watching the road leading to the valley, regularly inspected the entrances to the tombs to check that the seals, affixed at the moment of burial, were unbroken. Unfortunately, quite early all these precautions turned out to be useless. In fact, during a difficult and insecure period of political and social instability like the one that occurred at the end of Ramesses III's reign and that worsened until the end of the Twentieth Dynasty, the great amount of treasures heaped up in the tombs attracted ever more frequent robberies and pillages. It was therefore decided not to use that site any longer, since by then it was too well-known to the thieves and the pillagers. The priests removed the royal mummies to safer and better concealed places (such as the Deir el-Bahri cache), in order to save them from profanation. From the papyruses concerning the robberies in the tombs at the time of the Twentieth Dynasty, such as "Papyrus Mayer B", "Papyrus Salt 124" and "Papyrus Abbott", we learn that already at that time many private and royal tombs had been violated: the tomb of Tutankhamun represents a happy exception, having been covered up by debris from the excavation of the tomb of Ramesses IV, located above its entrance. Silence fell on the valley for many centuries, until the Ptolemaic era, when the first Greek and Roman

"tourists" arrived: the historian Diodorus Siculus, who was in Egypt in 57 BC writes: "They say that these are the tombs of the ancient kings: they are magnificent and they do not leave to posterity the possibility of creating anything more beautiful"; and on the walls of the tomb of Ramesses IV, for example, may be seen numerous graffiti left by the tourists of the Roman period. Then silence again descended on this sacred site, until the times of the Jesuit Claude Sicard, who was in Egypt between 1708 and 1712 and identified the site of ancient Thebes, rediscovering the tombs in the Valley of the Kings. Afterwards, in 1734, the English clergyman Richard Pococke visited the valley and drew its first plan, in which eighteen tombs appeared, only half of which were accessible. Later on, the Scotsman James Bruce explored the tomb of Ramesses III in 1768 and the scholars following Napoleon's 1798 expedition discovered the tomb of Amenophis III (WV no. 22) in the Western Valley and undertook the first scientific survey of the site.

16 top left James Bruce of Kinnaird, the great Scots traveler, visited Egypt in 1768 and 1769 and was among the first Europeans who went to the Valley of the Kings, where he was struck by a bas-relief decorating the wall of a tomb and representing two harpists. Bruce called this tomb, later referred to also as the "Tomb of Bruce", by the name of "Tomb of the Harpists": the tomb was subsequently identified by Champollion with that of Pharaoh Ramesses III (KV no. 11).

16 top right Bruce drew the bas-relief of the harpists which fascinated him so much, thus performing the first survey of a scene depicted in a royal tomb.

16 bottom The first drawing of the Valley of the Kings was published by the Reverend Pococke in 1734.

16-17 The Valley of the Kings in a famous lithograph by David Roberts, one of the leading British orientalist painters of the nineteenth century, who traveled to Egypt and to the Near East in 1838-9.

17 top
The two harpists of the Tomb of Bruce in a sketch executed by John Gardner Wilkinson, who traveled to Egypt between 1824 and 1836, visiting all the great archaeological sites and publishing numerous books, *among which is a monumental work called* Manners and Customs of the Ancient Egyptians. *To Wilkinson we owe the first numbering of the tombs in the Valley of the Kings.*

17 bottom
Jean François Champollion and Ippolito Rosellini visited the Valley of the Kings in 1828, identifying for the first time numerous tombs, among them the tomb Bruce had identified *as belonging to pharaoh Ramesses III. Champollion was the first to identify the Valley of the Kings as the necropolis of the Theban Pharaohs of the New Kingdom.*

Several years later, in 1817, Giovanni Battista Belzoni from Padua discovered the tombs of Ramesses I (KV no. 16), of Sethos I (KV no. 17) and of Ay, this last one in the Western Valley (WV no. 23). These exceptional discoveries were followed, three years later, by those of the Englishman James Burton, who discovered two uninscribed tombs and a third one (KV no. 5) assigned to Prince Meriatum "He Who is Loved by Atum, Son of Ramesses II".

Between 1824 and 1830, in the years following the decipherment of hieroglyphic writing, John Gardiner Wilkinson tenaciously worked in the Valley of the Kings, identifying and assigning for the first time to the tombs a numeration still in use today. In the years between 1828 and 1850 the valley was the goal of scientists, travelers and artists among whom were Champollion and Rosellini, Robert Hay, and Richard Lepsius, but new discoveries were not registered until 1898, when the Frenchman Victor Loret discovered two new tombs belonging to Tuthmosis III (KV no. 34) and Amenophis II (KV no. 35) and, in the next year the far smaller and more modest tomb of Tuthmosis I (KV no. 38). Finally, in 1903, Howard Carter discovered the tomb of Tuthmosis IV (KV no. 43) and in 1905 Theodore Davis discovered the untouched tomb of Yuya and Tuyu (KV no. 46), the parents of Queen Tiy, Amenophis III's wife. In that same period Edward Ayrton discovered the tombs of Pharaoh Siptah (KV no. 47) and of Horemheb (KV no. 57), the last ruler of the Eighteenth Dynasty.

18 top Giovanni Battista Belzoni, born in Padua in 1778, was one of the greatest travelers and explorers of Egypt in the period preceding the decipherment of the hieroglyphs. Belzoni reached Egypt in 1815 and remained there until 1819, linking his name to exceptional undertakings such as the opening of the temple of Abu Simbel and of the pyramid of Chephren.

18 bottom The plan of the Valley of the Kings drawn by Belzoni, emphasizing in black the tombs he discovered. To Belzoni, who operated in the Valley of the Kings in 1817, we owe, among other things, the discovery of the tomb of Ramesses I (KV no. 16), the tomb of Sethos I (KV no. 17), subsequently called "Belzoni's Tomb", and the tomb of Ay (WV no. 23) in the Western Valley.

19 top right Survey of the famous astronomic ceiling of the sarcophagus hall in the tomb of Sethos I, published in London in 1820 in a large album containing 44 watercolors for the illustration of the book written by Belzoni Narrative of the Operations and Recent Discoveries... in which the traveler drew up the report of his extraordinary adventure in Egypt.

19 top left
The cartouche with the praenomen of Sethos I, Menmaatre Sethos.

19 bottom left
Study executed by Alessandro Ricci of one of the pillars of what Belzoni called "the Hall of Beauties" in the tomb of Sethos I, showing the king in the presence of the goddess Hathor.

Alessandro Ricci from Siena, a physician and a great draftsman, worked in Egypt alongside of Belzoni, greatly contributing to surveying of the surveys of Sethos I's huge tomb.

19 bottom right
An original, unedited survey by Belzoni and Ricci executed in the tomb of Sethos I: Belzoni was the first to carry out a complete survey of the wall paintings in a tomb of the Valley of the Kings. The fruit of this huge work was shown to the public in an enormously successful exhibition in London in 1821 and repeated later in Paris, in which the two most beautiful halls of Sethos I's tomb were reconstructed.

A few years later, in 1922, Carter discovered the last royal tomb of the valley, the only royal burial site that had remained practically untouched: the very famous one of Tutankhamun (KV no. 62). The most recent discovery occurred in February 1995, when Kent Weeks of the American University in Cairo found a series of new rooms arranged for the sons of Ramesses II in the tomb located opposite that of Ramesses II (KV no. 5) already visited by Burton in 1820, of which practically every trace had

20 top left George Edward Stanhope Molyneux Herbert, fifth Earl of Carnarvon, the English aristocratic patron of the arts who agreed to finance the researches of an unemployed and practically unknown archaeologist by the name of Howard Carter. Carnarvon obtained the concession for the

Valley of the Kings in 1914, but the excavations started only in 1917, owing to the outbreak of World War I. On April 5, 1923, Lord Carnarvon died under mysterious and dramatic circumstances that gave birth to the legend of the "curse of the pharaohs".

20 bottom left Photograph of the tomb of Tutankhamun (KV no. 62) taken shortly after the discovery that took place on November 4, 1922. The tomb was located right below the tomb of Ramesses VI (at the center of the photo) and its entrance had been providentially concealed by the huge bulk of the debris produced by the digging of this last-mentioned burial site.

20 bottom right A train of workmen carries baskets of rubble away from a trench excavation of the tomb of Tutankhamun. The tomb included over 3,500 articles, and the emptying of the antechamber alone took some 50 days; the last objects were removed from the tomb only in 1930.

20-21 The doors of the second of the four huge shrines of gilded wood that contained the royal sarcophagi still carried the necropolis seal, unequivocal sign that the pharaoh's mummy was still intact, although the outmost shrine had been opened.

21 bottom left
On February 17, 1923, Carter (at the center) officially started the work for the opening of the burial chamber.

21 top right Carter with his trusted associate Arthur Callender and two workmen removing the walled structure that separated the antechamber from the burial chamber so as to be able to take out the wooden shrines containing the sarcophagi.

21 center right
One of the two statues posted to watch the sepulchral hall is being carefully wrapped up before being carried outside the tomb. The wooden statues, painted with a black resin, were provided with gold leaf covering the headdress and the triangular tunic, on which were found the pharaoh's cartouches, and they probably represented the royal ka.

21 bottom right
The northern wall of the antechamber partially demolished in order to allow access to the burial chamber, inside which the outer shrine of gilded wood containing the sarcophagi can be seen. On both sides of the wall, next to the door jambs, were found two life-sized wooden statues meant to protect the king's eternal rest.

22 top Numerous models of boats were found in the small room annexed to the burial chamber and called by Carter the "Treasury", in which there was also the shrine of the canopic vases. In the foreground can be seen the model of a sailing-boat resting on a wooden model of a granary.

22 center left An image of the goddess Hathor, represented with a cow's head and with a linen cloth around her neck, was found in the "Treasury" in front of the shrine of the canopic vases and behind a wooden statue of Anubis, already removed when this photograph was taken. On the left side several small boxes of painted wood can be seen, which contained jewels and other objects of funerary furniture.

22 center right In the antechamber we can see the pharaoh's four dismantled chariots and two of the three large ritual couches of gilded wood intended for the rest of the king's soul, over which were found several caskets of painted wood. Under the second couch can be distinguished several oval containers covered with white stucco, inside which were found food offerings for the feeding of the deceased pharaoh.

since been lost. This new section of the tomb, prepared for the sons of Ramesses II, fundamentally changes our knowledge of Ramessid tomb architecture and makes this strange tomb with a "T" plan and a series of 67 rooms found until now (which may increase following the exploration of a lower floor) the largest of all the valley's tombs.

22-23 After opening the second anthropoid coffin of gilded wood, by lifting its cover with the help of a complicated system of pulleys, the third coffin appeared, of solid gold, containing the pharaoh's mummy. Like the preceding one, the third coffin was covered with a linen shroud on which a wreath of flowers, leaves and fruits had been placed, but the whole was impregnated with a blackish solidified ointment.

23 top Carter cleans up the second coffin, of gilded wood inlaid with colored glass, after having gently removed the very thin linen cloth that covered it and on which had been laid festoons of flowers and of olive leaves.

22 bottom Howard Carter, in the foreground, is busy carefully wrapping up one of the two sentry statues posted on the northern wall of the antechamber, before their transfer to the nearby warehouse-laboratory. Contrary to the practice of many archaeologists of the time, Carter documented with great accuracy each stage of the emptying of the tomb, which therefore proceeded rather slowly.

23 bottom left A little wooden chapel found in the "Treasury" contained three small ritual gilded wooden statues of the king, covered with linen shrouds. The first small statue depicts Tutankhamun walking, while the two inner statues portray him on a papyrus boat in the act of hunting Seth's hippopotamus with a harpoon, evoking the myth of the fight that set Horus against Seth.

23 bottom right Carter and Callender open the doors of the four shrines of gilded wood containing the royal coffins. The doors of the first shrine did not carry seals, having perhaps been tampered with by the thieves who broke into the tomb in antiquity, without however succeeding in plundering it, but the doors of the second and the third shrines were still intact.

THE BUILDING OF
A ROYAL TOMB

The building of his own tomb, the place where the transformation and regeneration of the deceased king occurred, was one of the living pharaoh's deepest concerns. Generally, the location of the future tomb was chosen during the first year of his reign and a plan was worked out in which not only the architectural details were specified, but also the decorations – the paintings and the texts to be represented on the walls.

Their subsequent implementation was entrusted to the architect and to the craftsmen who lived in the village of Deir el-Medina and went to work following a trail over the mountain's crest that can still be easily crossed today (See itinerary no. 2).

The working days were of variable length, according to the tomb's dimensions, which in turn were proportional, at least within certain limits, to the duration of the reign. The working day started at dawn and lasted eight hours, with a break for lunch after the first four hours of work. The pace of work was therefore not exhausting, and during the working week, (lasting ten days)

25 top right On this little ostracon, preserved at the Fitzwilliam Museum in Cambridge, a workman can be seen using ordinary instruments.

25 center This large brush was probably used to spread the tomb walls with a thin plaster made of clay and limestone, with the final coating made up of a mixture of chalk and water. (Egyptian Museum, Turin)

25 bottom To draw straight lines the ancients made use of small wooden sticks to which were attached fine cords, whose imprint in some cases can still be seen today. (Egyptian Museum, Turin)

there were two rest days. To these weekly holidays many others were added on the occasion of the numerous religious festivities, and leaves of absence for personal or family reasons, occurring rather frequently, were also granted.

The craftsmen were organized in teams working under the supervision of an architect. Each team was divided into two groups, the right and the left, working simultaneously under the orders of two foremen in the respective parts of the tomb. The head of the team, originally appointed by the pharaoh himself or by the vizier (a dignitary acting as a prime minister), was directly responsible for the work, checked the reasons for the absences of the workmen, and had dealings with the vizier himself through a scribe specifically entrusted with this duty. The scribes, who fulfilled a highly important and prestigious role in Egyptian society, were also charged with the withdrawal from the pharaoh's warehouses of the food distributed as wages to the workmen, with the settling of quarrels, and with the administration of justice in the village of Deir el-Medina. The foremen, on the other hand, had to inspect the distribution of the material kept in the warehouses and record who was present and who absent. The groups did not have a fixed number of members, but the average strength was between 30 and 60 persons: this figure, however, could increase up to 120 persons if need be.

The workmen's duties were specialized and complementary: stone-cutters, plasterers, sculptors, draftsmen and decorators worked side by side and simultaneously in a sort of assembly line. The quarrymen came into operation first and, while the digging went on, penetrating always deeper inside the mountain, the plasterers smoothed the walls of the parts not too far from the surface, affixing a layer of *muna*, a kind of plaster obtained from a mixture of clay and quartz, limestone and crushed straw, over which were laid thinner layers of clay and limestone, successively whitened with a layer of gypsum dissolved in water.

The execution of the decorative program, chosen by the high priests in agreement with the pharaoh, was entrusted to the draftsmen. These worked using a red ochre, after having subdivided the surface to paint into numerous squares, by means of a string fastened to a stick, in order to be able to place correctly the figures and the texts and make sure that proportions were in accordance with very precise rules. The draftsmen were under the supervision of a chief draftsman, who made necessary corrections using black charcoal. Then the sculptors stepped in and started carving the rock to obtain a bas-relief, to be colored later by the painters, who used six basic colors with precise symbolic and ritual meanings.

ARCHITECTURE AND DECORATION OF THE TOMBS

26 top The painters, proceeding to the final stage of the decoration, used small palettes, similar to these preserved in the Cairo Museum.

The plan of the royal tombs is complex, and each tomb has a peculiar physiognomy of its own, even though there generally are constant elements such as the stairway, the descending corridor off which halls open, and the burial chamber designed to contain the pharaoh's sarcophagus.

An important architectural peculiarity distinguishes the tombs of the Eighteenth Dynasty from those of the Nineteenth (even though some exceptions are known): in the first the descending corridor generally forms a 90° bend before penetrating into the sarcophagus hall, while in the second it proceeds in a straight line. This tendency to a linear development along the major axis

becomes still more evident in the tombs of the Twentieth Dynasty and was probably related to a change in religious conceptions, according to which the tomb's structure itself had somehow to reflect the trajectory of the solar star.

As to the wall decorations, the scenes represented never dealt with aspects of everyday life, or with historical-biographical elements, but only with the Afterlife and the trip the pharaoh had to undertake – overcoming numerous trials – in order to reach the kingdom of Osiris.

The style of the decorations varies from imitations of papyrus to elaborate and painted bas-reliefs, but the subjects remain overall the same: the texts painted on the walls are taken from the great magical-religious anthologies of the time – such as the *Book of the Dead*, the *Book of Amduat*, the *Book of Gates*, the *Book of Caverns*, the *Book of Earth*, and the *Litanies of Re* – and are generally illustrated with scenes related to them, to ensure the deceased had the requisite knowledge of the magic formulas needed to overcome the hardships he would face. In fact, for the ancient Egyptians, the tomb had a totally different meaning than it has today. It had a "sacred architecture" and a sacred orientation of its own, which did not coincide at all with the geographical and terrestrial ones: in it the deceased accomplishes a ritual journey. The deceased descends to the kingdom of the dead, symbolized by the tomb, overcomes the numerous obstacles standing in his way (using the appropriate magic formulas prescribed in the *Book of the Dead)*, and is introduced by kindly divinities into the kingdom of Osiris, Lord of the Afterlife, symbolized by the hall of the sarcophagus.

This hall, called by the Egyptians the "golden hall", referring to the gold that represents the incorruptible flesh of the gods, was the spot where was supposed to take place the pharaoh's transformation into a divine entity, whose soul "came out to the light" – that is, climbed to the sky in order to be reunited with the sun-god Re, his divine father.

26 center
The decorative plan of the royal tombs was established in detail by the priests and it concerned exclusively the world of the Afterlife, the journey the deceased pharaoh had to accomplish in order to reach the kingdom of Osiris, guided by texts taken from the great magical-religious anthologies of the time. The photograph shows a detail of the decoration of the western wall of the burial chamber of Tutankhamun's tomb (KV no. 62), illustrating a passage of the Book of Amduat.

26 bottom After the sculptors had modeled the tomb's wall by incising the rock with metal points, generally using the bas-relief technique, the surfaces were further smoothed and colored by decorator-painters.

27 top The tomb had its precise geographical and ritual orientations, related to the decorative plan, and sometimes on the walls of the tomb under construction the workmen drew the symbols of the cardinal points, as can be noticed in the burial chamber of Horemheb's tomb (KV no. 57). The photograph shows the symbol of the West.

The pigments used in the tombs

While the digging went on in the deepest parts of the tomb, the external parts were practically finished. This rational organization allowed work to proceed at an incredible speed and, even though the tombs were dug with rather rudimentary tools, a royal tomb could be completed within a few months, though in the case of the larger and more complex tombs a variable period of some six to ten years was required.

The sons of the craftsmen were also employed in the work, being entrusted with simple and not very wearisome tasks. These boys used to work hoping to become in their turn "servants in the Seat of Truth", as Deir el-Medina craftsmen were referred to at the time.

Side by side with all these persons were the serfs – simple laborers provided to the craftsmen's community by the pharaoh and entrusted with the humblest and the more tiresome labors necessary to the functioning of the groups of specialized workmen, such as, the carrying of water, the preparing of plaster, and the preparing of torches for lighting. The torches were made of baked clay containers filled with oil of sesame and salt or with animal fat and salt, inside which floated a twisted linen taper. It seems that salt was used to prevent the combustion releasing smoke, which would have harmed the paintings.

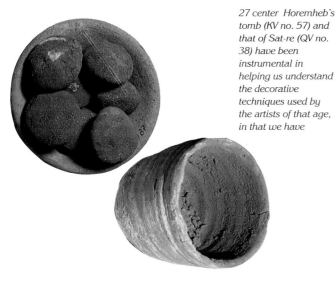

27 center Horemheb's tomb (KV no. 57) and that of Sat-re (QV no. 38) have been instrumental in helping us understand the decorative techniques used by the artists of that age, in that we have incomplete walls left in different working stages. It is thus possible to see how the primitive red ochre sketch was being corrected with black charcoal.
At this stage the sculptors stepped in, carving the surface of the rock and then whitewashing it with water and chalk before handing over to the painters.

THE PIGMENTS USED IN THE TOMBS

COLOR	PIGMENT	SYMBOLIC MEANING	NOTES
white	gypsum - huntite	represents silver	used also as background
blue	cuprorivaite or Egyptian blue	symbolizes the sky and the body of the celestial divinities	obtained artificially by synthesis
yellow	yellow ochre - orpiment	represents gold, gods' flesh; expresses the idea of preciousness	used also as background. Orpiment was imported from Asia
black	coal	death and eternal preservation	
red	red ochre	fire and blood	easily found in the clay formations of the Theban mountain
green	copper wollastonite	regeneration	artificially obtained by synthesis

27 bottom Red and blue were colors widely employed in the decoration of the tombs, but their origins were quite different. The red color was generally obtained by grinding red ochres containing iron oxide, while the blue was a synthetic color – the first synthetic color in history – produced by heating at over 700°C a mixture of copper salts, calcium and sand mixed with a flux (sodium salts).

THE BURIAL OF THE PHARAOH

The news of the pharaoh's death was generally received with a degree of joy by the Deir el-Medina craftsmen, not just because the enthroning of a new king meant new work, but also because it was necessary quickly to put the final touches to the tomb and to the very numerous funerary furnishings that had to accompany the king in his last dwelling – operations that all offered opportunities for additional income. Generally there was a three-month interval between the king's death and his burial: the time needed for the complex ritual of the embalming and preparation of the king's corpse. This, after having been immersed for 70 days in natron, was wrapped in a first layer of very thin linen bandages on which were laid, in well-determined spots, numerous amulets. It was later covered with a second layer of broader bandages soaked in resin and aromatic essential oils.

The procession, setting out from the royal palace, reached the West of Thebes and entered "the Road where Re Sets" heading for "the Great and Majestic Necropolis of the Pharaoh's Millions of Years Life Strength Health in the West of Thebes". The royal mummy in its wooden sarcophagus was followed by parties of women screaming and crying, while the bald-headed priests burned incense and shook their sistrums.

As it reached the tomb and faced it, the coffin was stood upright and the high priest, or sometimes, the new pharaoh, accomplished the ritual of the "Opening of the Mouth", thanks to which the deceased magically reacquired the use of his mouth and was able to speak again, to drink and to eat. Then the mortal remains were carried to the burial chamber, where a monumental stone sarcophagus had been prepared long since, on which was laid a heavy cover carved in high relief with the king's image. At that time, while family and friends started the funerary banquet, the workmen hermetically closed the entrance to the tomb, on which the necropolis seals were affixed.

The entrance was not always hidden but, mainly starting from the Nineteenth Dynasty, was left in plain view; the necropolis guards, beside garrisoning the road leading to the valley, regularly inspected the seals in order to verify their integrity, after which they drew up careful reports. Once the tomb was closed and sealed, nobody was permitted to penetrate it anymore and the valley itself was a forbidden spot where only the craftsmen and the guards were entitled to go: the worship of the deceased king never required a return to the place of burial and was performed far away, in the plain of the Nile Valley in the "temples of millions of years" where the king united with eternity in the estates of Amun in the West of Thebes.

28 top right The seals were of two kinds: a first kind was impressed in the plaster of the doors, while a second kind was affixed on a small clay block around the fine cords with which the doors of the shrines containing the sarcophagi or the canopic vases were closed.

28 top left Seals were placed on the necropolis by officials responsible for the security of the tombs. Different types were used, but they generally included the figure of Anubis, who appeared as a crouched jackal. In some cases the royal scroll was depicted at the side and, underneath, a number of prisoners (nine or, less frequently, four) tied with their hands behind their backs and sometimes beheaded.

-29 This scene, depicted on the east wall of the burial chamber of the tomb of Tutankhamun (KV no. 62), shows the coffin of the dead king, placed in a shrine and mounted on a sleigh. It is being pulled along by twelve high dignitaries, among them the viziers of Upper and Lower Egypt, distinguishable from the others by the style of their tunic which leaves their right shoulder bare. As the hieroglyphs tell us, they are chanting in unison: "O Nebkheprure, come in peace, O god protector of the earth."

The tombs of the Valley of the Kings

Out of the 62 tombs known today in the Valley of the Kings, only about 20 actually sheltered pharaohs: indeed, many were abandoned because the workmen came up against unsuitable rock formations, some were only undecorated corridors with little rooms in the back, while others were used for various members of the royal family.

Among the royal tombs, fifteen are generally open to the public, even though several of them may temporarily be closed for restoration works, rendered increasingly necessary both by the influx of a considerable crowd of tourists, whose very presence, unintentionally upsets the sensitive microclimate of these monuments, and by the unstable hydrogeological conditions of the valley itself. Since a complete description of all the tombs of the Valley of the Kings that can be visited would require much more space than is available in this introductory guide, we shall of necessity make a choice based upon criteria of artistic value and general interest.

DYNASTIES	KV n. tomb	Date of discovery	Discoverer	Length (meters)
EIGHTEENTH DYNASTY				
Tuthmosis I	38	1899	Loret	25
Tuthmosis II	42 ?	1900	Carter	50
Hatshepsut	20	1903	Carter	200
Tuthmosis III	34	1898	Loret	55
Amenophis II	35	1898	Loret	60
Tuthmosis IV	43	1903	Carter	90
Amenophis III	WV 22	1799	Jollois/Devillier	100
Tutankhamun	62	1922	Carter	40
Ay	WV 23	1816	Belzoni	55
Horemheb	57	1908	Ayrton	114
NINETEENTH DYNASTY				
Ramesses I	16	1817	Belzoni	29
Sethos I	17	1817	Belzoni	100
Ramesses II	7	antiquity		100
Merneptah	8	antiquity		115
Sethos II	15	?		72
Amenemesses	10	1907	Ayrton	75
Siptah	47	1905	Ayrton	90
Twosret	14	antiquity		110
TWENTIETH DYNASTY				
Sethenakhte	14	antiquity		110
Ramesses III	11	antiquity		125
Ramesses IV	2	antiquity		66
Ramesses VI / V	9	antiquity		104
Ramesses VII	1	antiquity		40
Ramesses IX	6	antiquity		86
Ramesses X	18	?		40
Ramesses XI	4	antiquity		93

28 bottom left
The iconographic documentation of the royal funerary ritual is rather scanty, although the scenes showing the funerary ritual in private tombs are more numerous.
In this wall painting we see the priest performing a cleansing in front of the coffin of the deceased, standing upright at the tomb door before proceeding to the ceremony of the "Opening of the Mouth".

29 top left A peculiar moment of the funerary ritual was the ceremony of the "Opening of the Mouth", in which the officiating priest magically restored to the deceased the use of speech and senses. In this scene, painted on the northern wall of Tutankhamun's tomb (KV no. 62), it is the pharaoh Ay, dressed as a sem-priest, who performs the ceremony of the "Opening of the Mouth" in front of Tutankhamun, shown as Osiris.

29 top right In this scene, painted in Sennedjem's tomb (TT no. 1), Anubis, "the Divine Embalmer", is bent over the deceased's body while performing his skills. Anubis was not only the protector of the necropolis but also, according to tradition, the inventor of the embalming process, which was placed under his guardianship.

TOMBS OF THE EIGHTEENTH DYNASTY

TUTHMOSIS III
1479 - 1425 BC

KV no. 34

TUTHMOSIS

MENKHEPERRE

The tomb of Tuthmosis III is located in a narrow gorge at the bottom of the Valley of the Kings, a fold of the rocky wall forming the flank of the main wadi, which has to be climbed on a small metal ladder in order to reach the tomb's entrance, some 30 meters above ground level.

The tomb of the great pharaoh, who officially mounted the throne rather young, at the death of Tuthmosis II, but was able to assume power only at the death of Hatshepsut, his father's sister (who at first undertook the regency and later succeeded in having herself enthroned), was discovered in 1898 by Victor Loret, then director of the Antiquities Service. An exceptional ruler, considered, along with Ramesses II, to be one of Egypt's greatest pharaohs, Tuthmosis III, besides being a very great strategist who led glorious military campaigns in the East, consolidating a huge empire, was an innovator in the religious field, as he knew how to recover the tradition of the ancient Heliopolitan worships. It was under his reign that the Valley of the Kings definitely assumed the character of a royal necropolis.

Despite its position, which rendered it almost inaccessible,the tomb did not escape looting by the necropolis robbers and was found by Loret deprived of great artistic treasures but still with part of its funerary furniture.

The tomb begins with a double succession of steps and a corridor. The second corridor leads to a rectangular shaft which in turn ends in a two-pillar vestibule, at 90° to the corridor axis and decorated with reproductions of the 765 divinities that daily generate the sun. The purpose of the shaft – a structure

found in many, though not all, of the royal tombs – is subject to debate, but it is highly probable that the shafts had above all a ritual meaning, as an evocation of the cavern of Sokar, a very ancient funerary deity, protectress of the deceased king. They possibly also had the practical aim of physically protecting the sarcophagus hall, both from desecration and from flooding following torrential rains. From the vestibule, a few steps lead into the oval-shaped burial chamber, with two pillars at the center and four lateral annexes opening off the eastern and the western sides.

The large burial chamber, holding a wonderful sarcophagus of red quartzite on which is carved an image of the goddess Nut, was conceived as a huge ornamental scroll inside which

the complete texts of the *Book of Amduat* were written as on a papyrus, while on the pillars there are passages taken from the *Litanies of Re*. By the name of *Book of Amduat* (this last word meaning "that which there is in the Afterlife"), we refer today to a collection of magical and religious texts called by the ancient Egyptians the *Book of the Secret Room*, subdivided into twelve parts corresponding to the night's twelve hours and dealing with Afterlife's sacred geography and with the sun's nightly course. The *Amduat* is the oldest of all the texts transcribed on the tomb walls of the Valley of the Kings. Tuthmosis III's mummy was found in 1881 inside tomb no. 320 at Deir el-Bahri.

34 This miniature model is a small-scale but extremely accurate reproduction of the second coffin. Found with three other identical ones inside the canopic shrine made of calcite, it contained the viscera of the king (his intestines, to be precise) and had been placed under the protection of Qebhsenuef, one of the four sons of Horus. (Cairo Museum)

35 left The second coffin, also referred to as the intermediate coffin, of gilded laminated wood with inlays of polychrome glass pastes. The coffin cover was attached by ten silver strips, each kept in place by as many silver nails. (Cairo Museum)

35 right The famous gold mask weighing ten kilos that rested directly on the pharaoh's mummy inside the third coffin. The pharaoh wears the classic nemes headdress striped with transversal bands of glass paste imitating lapis lazuli, and is adorned with a wide collar composed of streaks of semiprecious stones and colored glasses, while the eyes are of quartz and obsidian. (Cairo Museum)

BURIAL CHAMBER

TREASURY

a

↑ N

CORRIDOR

ANTECHAMBER

STAIRWAY

ANNEXE

a - Funerary procession, "Opening of the Mouth", scenes with deities and Book of Amduat

A - The three ritual beds of gilded wood were decorated with the effigies of three deities: Isis Mehet (lion-headed), Meheret Weret, (cow-headed), with lyre-shaped horns framing a solar disk (in the photo), and Ammit, (a creature made up of a hippopotamus head and a crocodile's body). (Cairo Museum)

B - This small wooden naos covered with a gold lamina mounted on a sledge was found in the antechamber and was probably meant to contain a little statue of the king, removed during the episodes of partial plundering of the tomb in antiquity. The walls of the naos are decorated with splendid scenes of hunting and of daily life. (Cairo Museum)

C - The so-called "ecclesiastic throne" of ebony with gold inlays, semiprecious stones and polychrome glass pastes was found in the annex. In the texts painted on the back panel, whose upper part is decorated with an Amarnan-type solar disk, the pharaoh is quoted both with his original name of Tutankhaten and with the later and better known one of Tutankhamun. (Cairo Museum)

D - Tutankhamun's royal throne is, after the mortuary mask, the best-known object found in the tomb. The throne of engraved wood is covered with sheet gold and adorned with semiprecious stones and polychrome glass pastes. Its back panel is decorated with a beautiful scene strongly influenced by the Amarna style, in which the royal spouse, Ankhesenamun, can be seen standing in front of the pharaoh and resting her hand on his shoulder; a solar disk, a reminder of the Aten cult, spreads its rays on the royal couple. (Cairo Museum)

ANNEXE

ANTECHAMBER

DESCENDING CORRIDOR

E - One of the two wooden and painted sentry-statues posted in the antechamber at the sides of the walled door that led into the burial chamber: these life-sized statues were a figuration of the royal ka. (Cairo Museum)

F - The third coffin, made of solid gold.

G - The burial chamber as it appears today, with the large red quartzite sarcophagus containing the first wooden coffin and the king's mummy. On the background wall Tutankhamun is shown with his ka facing Osiris, and the ceremony of the "Opening of the Mouth" is celebrated by his successor, Ay. (Cairo Museum)

H - The gilded-wood canopic shrine.

I - In the antechamber in front of the shrine of the canopic chest was found a statue of Anubis, originally covered with a linen cloth, on a little chapel of gilded wood mounted on a palanquin so that it might be carried during the funeral procession. (Cairo Museum)

F

G

H

TREASURY

BURIAL CHAMBER

N

38 left and top right
Tutankhamun – originally called Tutankhaten, was the son of Amenophis IV/ Akhenaten, the heretic pharaoh who enforced the worship of Aten, the sole solar god, moving the state's capital from Thebes to Amarna.
Tutankhamun, a name meaning "the Living Image of Amun", mounted the throne in 1333 BC, assuming the praenomen of Nebkheprure, and in year 2 of the reign changed his name from Tutankhaten to Tutankhamun. He died in year 9 or perhaps 10 of his reign at the age of about seventeen, in circumstances that have yet to be elucidated. Before the discovery of his tomb, Tutankhamun was a practically unknown pharaoh. (Cairo Museum)

38 bottom right
The large sarcophagus of red quartzite, inside which were the three anthropoid coffins, is still in the tomb today. It was adorned on the corners with the images of four protecting deities with outspread wings: Nephthys (in the photograph), Isis, Selkis and Neith.

FIRST ANTHROPOID
COFFIN (WOOD)

SECOND ANTHROPOID
COFFIN (WOOD)

THIRD ANTHROPOID
COFFIN (SOLID GOLD)

GOLDEN MASK

MUMMY OF
TUTANKHAMUN

RED QUARTZITE
SARCOPHAGUS

39 top right Vertical plan of Tutankhamun's coffins and shrines.

39 bottom The third coffin, of solid gold weighing about 110 kilos, contained the royal mummy. In all three anthropoid coffins the king is represented in an identical way: with the nemes *headdress and the ceremonial beard and folding his arms as his hands grasp the insignia of the royal power – the* heqa-scepter *in the left and the* nekhakha-*flail in the right. From the king's forehead a snake and a vulture stand out, emblems of Wadjet and Nekhbet, the two tutelary deities of Lower and Upper Egypt. (Cairo Museum)*

40 top Extremely refined scenes of hunting and of the sovereign's daily life inspired by the Amarnan style, decorate the walls of this little naos about 50 centimeters high found in the annex. Tutankhamun is shown hunting with the royal spouse, Ankhesenamun. In the lower scene, the king sits on a high-backed chair and shoots with a bow at the birds rising in flight from a thicket of papyruses, while his wife holds out an arrow to him. (Cairo Museum)

40 bottom left Gilded wood statuette of Sokar, a funeral divinity in the form of a falcon, whose role was to protect the dead. This statuette was one of a group of 32 found in the "Treasury", most of them depicting gods and goddesses. (Cairo Museum)

40 bottom right Detail of the third, solid-gold, coffin on which the goddess Isis is shown with her wings spread out in a protective attitude, as she appears to be embracing the mummy's feet. (Cairo Museum)

41 top left Golden fan decorated with a hunting scene: the pharaoh on his chariot, to which are attached two fiery horses "strong as bulls" – so goes the text – is hunting ostriches. Two servants carry on their shoulders birds already shot down. (Cairo Museum)

41 top right Short dagger with gold blade and a haft decorated with gold granulations and glass paste stripes and mounted semiprecious stones, reproducing floral motifs. On the sheath there are relief representetions of oryxes, of a cow, of a bull attacked by a dog and of a leopard. (Cairo Museum)

41 bottom left This gilded wood statuette portrays Tutankhamun hunting hippopotamus with a harpoon, from a boat made of papyrus. It is certainly the loveliest of the statuettes discovered in the "Treasury". Like all the others, it was wrapped in a linen cloth which left only the face showing. The scene depicted - in which the pharaoh, protector of order on Earth, spears the hippotamus, incarnation of chaos and evil powers - evokes the legendary fight of Horus against Seth. (Cairo Museum)

41 bottom right Gilded wood statuette of the lioness-goddess. Sekhmet, considered the consort of Ptah; her many duties included ensuring the protection of the king. (Cairo Museum)

42 top Pectoral in the shape of a falcon with its wings spread out and the head surmounted by a solar disk; the claws hold two shenu-signs, powerful protecting amulets related to the concept of eternity, surmounted by two ankh-signs, amulets related to the vital breath and to life. (Cairo Museum)

42 center Pectoral in the shape of a winged scarab with a solar disk resting on a neb-sign. The scarab, a beetle emerging from the earth as he pushes forward a little sand ball, evokes for the ancient Egyptians the image of the sun-god Re on his morning rising. The combination solar disk (Re) ⊙, scarab (khepru) 🪲 and neb-sign ⌣ allows the reading of the pharaoh's name – Nebkheprure. (Cairo Museum)

42 bottom left Earrings of gold and polychrome glass pastes with pendants. (Cairo Museum)

42 bottom right Alabaster cover of one of the four canopic jars modeled after the image of the king: the king's viscera were enclosed in four miniaturized coffins placed in four cells of a box, also made of alabaster, also each one of them closed with such a cover. (Cairo Museum)

43 top left Gold ointments holder in the shape of a double cartouche surmounted by solar disks and plumes with representations of the king, sitting on a large neb-sign, in the different moments of his life: young man, adult, deceased and after his rebirth. (Cairo Museum)

43 center Pectoral in the shape of a chapel with a vulture inside with its wings spread out, holding two shenu-signs in his claws, found by Carter in the annex. The analysis of the hieroglyphs, oriented in the cartouches in an unusual way, has led to the opinion that this jewel had originally been prepared for Pharaoh Akhenaten and was later reused by his son Tutankhamun. (Cairo Museum)

43 bottom left This object of outstanding beauty was found by Carter among the debris that partially obstructed the descending corridor; it shows a lotus flower carved in wood and painted, surmounted by the head of the pharaoh as a boy, evoking the rebirth of Tutankhamun, like the sun being born from the lotus. (Cairo Museum)

43 bottom right Unusual calcite model of a boat with double oryx-headed prow resting on a little alabaster basin. At the center of the boat a baldachin is supported by four double-capital pillars in the shape of lotus and papyrus, under which there is a kind of sarcophagus. At the stern a dwarfish woman steers the boat, while at the prow a naked young woman holds in her hand a lotus flower. The meaning of this object is not yet quite clear. (Cairo Museum)

43

AY
1324-1321 BC

WV no. 23

AY ITNETER

KHEPERKHEPERURE

A - Passages from the Book of Amduat in vertical columns of text: in the upper register there are a first boat with standards carrying the emblem of the falcon, the goddess Nephthys and the boat of the Ennead.

B - The entrance to the little room annexed to the burial chamber: above the architrave four deities can be seen (perhaps they are Horus's four sons) facing a table of offerings.

N

E

D

F

G

STAIRWAY

SECOND CORRIDOR

BURIAL CHAMBER

a

VESTIBULE

ANNEXE

H

C

B

A

C - Ay and his ka are in the presence of (from left to right) Osiris and the goddesses Hathor-Imentit, Nut (officiating the njnj rite and Hathor).

D, E - Sarcophagus of red quartzite analogous in shape and decorative program to that of Tutankhamun. At the corners the four tutelary deities are carved in relief: Isis, Nephthys, Selkis and Neith.

STAIRWAY

FIRST CORRIDOR

BURIAL CHAMBER

SECOND CORRIDOR

FIRST CORRIDOR

ANNEXE

VESTIBULE

STAIRWAY

STAIRWAY

N

F, G - Passages from the Book of Amduat, analogous to those in Tutankhamun's tomb, are transcribed and illustrated in the wall paintings of the sarcophagus hall. In the photograph,

Khepri's solar boat preceeded by five deities can be seen, and in the lower registers twelve baboon deities corresponding to the twelve hours of the night.

H - The pharaoh (the image is irremediably lost) on a papyrus boat is hunting birds in the marshes, using a hunting club.

a - Bird-hunting scenes, Book of Amduat and scenes with gods

The tomb of Ay, Tutankhamun's successor, who mounted the throne at the death of the young king whose authoritative counsellor and vizier he had been, is found in the Western Valley, whose entrance is located near the new rest-house of the Valley of the Kings. From here starts a track which, after passing close to Amenophis III's tomb (WV no. 22), follows the bottom of this wonderful and wild valley and after about two kilometers reaches Ay's tomb, which was recently opened to the public for the first time.

The tomb, which not only had already been looted in antiquity, but appears to have been the object of deliberate mutilation, was discovered in 1816 by Belzoni, who carved his name and the date on the rock at the side of the entrance: inside, he recovered only fragments of a sarcophagus, while the king's mummy was never found.

The tomb of Ay has a linear architectural structure that curiously seems to anticipate the typical plans of the Twentieth Dynasty's tombs; it includes a descending stairway leading to the first corridor and a second flight of steps giving access to the second corridor, which, in its turn, ends in a vestibule followed by the burial chamber, off which opens a small annex.

Even though quite damaged, the tomb is interesting both because it presents a beautiful bird-hunting scene in the marshes – an absolutely unique depiction for a royal tomb – and because it continues a decorative design already found in the tomb of Tutankhamun, featuring, for example, the representation of the twelve monkeys symbolizing the night hours on one of the burial chamber's walls. From this originates the name of *Bab el-Gurud*, "Tomb of the Baboons", given to the tomb by the natives and then, by extension, to the Western Valley: *Wadi el-Gurud*, namely "Valley of the Monkeys".

HOREMHEB
1321-1295 BC

KV no. 57

HOREMHEB MERIAMUN

DJESERKHEPERURE SETEPENRE

The tomb of Horemheb, Ay's successor, was discovered in February 1908 by the young British Egyptologist Edward Ayrton, who worked under orders from Theodore Davis, a wealthy American passionately fond of archaeology. As a result of its position the large tomb was full of debris, carried by the waters of the rushing torrents developing very quickly during the rare but torrential rains falling from to time in the region of Thebes.

Horemheb had served at Amenophis IV's court, and continued under Tutankhamun and finally under Ay, before himself ascending the throne. From a religious point of view Horemheb – royal scribe and general of the armies, on whom had also been bestowed the title of *erpa* (prince) and who, at the time of the Ramessids was regarded as Amenophis III's direct descendant – is essentially an energetic restorer of Amun's old worship. From a political point view he is a restructurer of the provincial administration and of the military cadres.

A great builder (he enlarged the Karnak temple, erecting the second, ninth and tenth pylons and dismantling the Aten temples in order to reuse their materials), he ordered the construction of a new tomb in the Valley of the Kings, as requested by tradition, even though he already had a high dignitary's tomb of his own at Saqqara.

With Horemheb, the Eighteenth Dynasty traditionally ends – even though, from the point of view of dynastic right, it had already ended several decades before with Tutankhamun, the last real royal-blood pharaoh of the Amenophis stock. However, one may also say that with Horemheb, a transition pharaoh, begins the Nineteenth Dynasty, and his tomb seems to reflect this major change.

The architectural structure of his tomb presents two stylistic innovations that will characterize the large Nineteenth Dynasty hypogea: the disappearance of the right angle between the end of the descending corridor and the vestibule preceding the burial chamber, and the introduction of painted bas-relief instead of simple painting in the decorations of the walls.

In addition, for the first time, passages from the *Book of Gates*, a religious composition (so called with reference to the "gates" that separate the night's twelve hours).

appear in the texts transcribed on the walls – an evolution from the *Book of Amduat*.

The first descending stairway ends in the first corridor, leading to a second stairway and a second corridor ending in a room with a shaft on whose walls appear the first paintings, showing two groups of deities: Hathor, Isis, Osiris and Horus to the left, and Hathor, Anubis, Osiris and Horus to the right. The tomb continues with a two-pillar hall from where the third corridor leads to the vestibule, which, in its turn, leads to the burial chamber, supported by six pillars. In the burial chamber, off which open four lateral and one back annex, a large sarcophagus, still in place, can be observed and, on a wall, a scene recalling the fifth division of the *Book of Gates* with the figure of Osiris into whose presence are carried nine personages.

One of the most interesting aspects of Horemheb's tomb is that many wall decorations were interrupted at different stages of the work, and thus give an exact idea of the techniques used by Deir el-Medina's artists. At certain points the drawings are just sketched; at others the grids used for calculating the proportions of the illustrations or the corrections of the chief artist can be seen; at others still the sculptor's work begins as he incises the plaster layer in order to obtain the bas-reliefs which will later be painted ... The fact that the tomb was not finished is all the more unusual if we realize that Horemheb had reigned for not less than 28 years – a period more than sufficient to complete the decoration of any tomb – and we almost have the impression that all of this had been done on purpose, as if to leave a message.

46 top Several parts of Horemheb's tomb were left unfinished at different stages of the decoration: in this case the painters were spreading the grey-blue background that characterizes this tomb. The reason for presence of these unfinished parts is obscure, particularly if we take into account that the tombs were being prepared in rather short spaces of time and that Horemheb reigned for about 30 years.

46-47 In this double scene located in the southeastern corner of the antechamber, Horemheb performs a wine offering to Anubis by holding out to him ritual nu-vases, while to the right the pharaoh stands between Hathor-Imentit and Harsiesis.

47 top left The pharaoh in the presence of Harsiesis, one the forms of the god Horus, "Son of Isis", represented in a falcon-headed human shape with the double crown of Upper and Lower Egypt.

47 top right In the scenes located on the western wall of the antechamber the pharaoh performs a ritual offering to Hathor-Imentit, then finds himself in the presence of Harsiesis and, successively, performs offerings to Isis and finally faces Anubis.

47 bottom General view of the antechamber: in the background to the sides of the door, the pharaoh can be seen in front of Hathor-Imentit, to the right, and between Hathor-Imentit and Harsiesis, to the left.

A - Detail of the astronomical ceiling of the six-pillar hall: in the blue background the yellow five-point stars symbolize the heavenly vault.

B - The texts in vertical columns reproduce passages from the Book of Gates, a magic-religious anthology used toward the end of the Eighteenth Dynasty, dealing with the twelve doors, corresponding to the night hours the sun has to cross. In the upper register the first hour of the Book of Gates is illustrated: ram-headed Re moves forward on his boat in the world of the Afterlife, hauled by four genies, while in the lower register the god Atum can be seen facing four men lying down, defined by the text as "those who are exhausted" – an embodiment of the four cardinal points (necessary only in the earthly world) – followed by the enemies of the light with their hands tied behind their back.

C - The sarcophagus of Horemheb, in red quarzite and similar in form to that of his predecessors Tutankhamun and Ay, was found open with the lid broken: inside were fragments of bone belonging to several people; it was impossible to identify those of the king.

A

C

B

N ←⊙

SIX-PILLAR
HALL

ANNEXE

c

ANNEXE

VESTIBULE

THIRD
CORRIDOR

STAIRWAY

b

ANNEXE

BURIAL
CHAMBER

ANNEXE

ANNEXE

D

E

F

D - A part of the wall remained unfinished and only the red and black marks drawn by the draftsmen and by the correctors can be seen.

E, F - Details of the western wall of the antechamber: the god Harsiesis, falcon-headed with the double crown of Upper and Lower Egypt, and the goddess Isis, here represented in a form analogous to Hathor's with two lyre-shaped horns framing a solar disk on her head.

G - Horemheb is taken by the hand by Anubis, who displays the classic attributes of the deities: the long was-scepter in his right hand and the ankh-cross in his left.

STAIRWAY

FIRST CORRIDOR

RITUAL SHAFT

SECOND CORRIDOR

-PILLAR ALL

G

a - Scenes with gods
b - Scenes with gods
c - Book of Gates

49 bottom
The pharaoh's cartouches transcribing his praenomen and his name: Djeserkheperure Horemheb. The praenomen was taken up by the pharaoh at the moment of his crowning, since it designated the king of Upper and Lower Egypt.

TOMBS OF THE NINETEENTH DYNASTY

RAMESSES I
1295-1294 BC

KV no. 16

A - This scene illustrates a passage of the Book of Gates reproduced in the vertical registers above the god Atum as he fights the malevolent snake Apophis.

B - The boat of Re, shown with a ram's head inside a tabernacle surrounded by the mehen-snake, moves ahead in the Afterlife, hauled by four deities (not visible in the photograph).

C - Iun-Mutef, dressed in the characteristic leopard-skin hide, faces the pharaoh and diverse deities (not seen in the photograph). The Iun-mutef, a name meaning "(Horus) Support of his Mother", is a form of Horus related to ancient priestly functions and was at the same time a priestly charge.

D - In the little niche opening off the southwestern wall of the burial chamber, a scene related to the third hour of the Book of Gates shows Osiris between a ram-headed deity and the snake goddess Nesert.

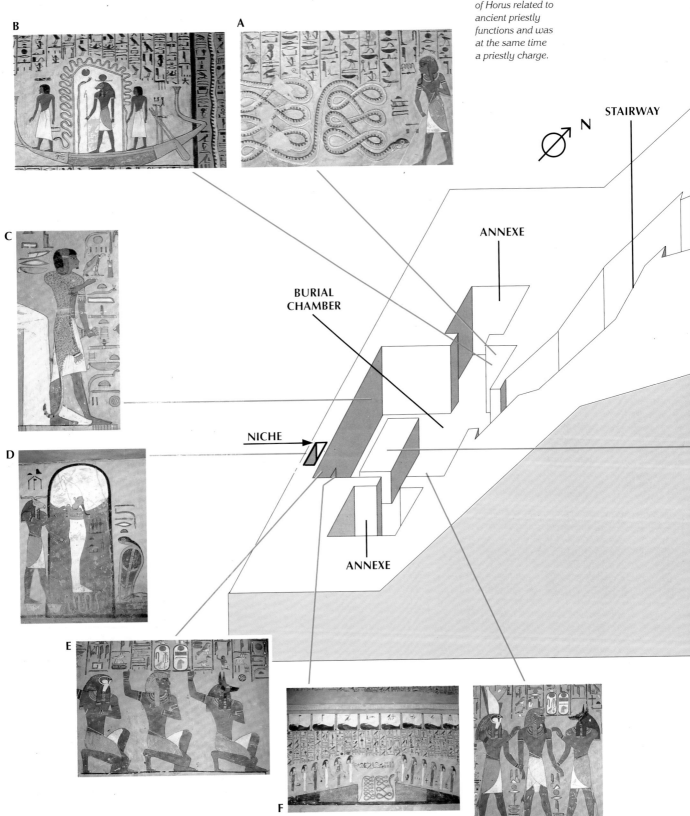

STAIRWAY

ANNEXE

BURIAL CHAMBER

NICHE

ANNEXE

E - The pharaoh, kneeling among the souls of the towns of Pe and of Nekhen, (ancient towns of the Delta and of Upper Egypt) embodying the souls of the deceased kings, performs the henu-gesture, which expresses prayer and joy.

F - The fourth hour of the Book of Gates*: above, nine mummies (in black anthropoid coffins) who will be revived by the passage of the solar boat. At the center, in a ditch, a snake with multiple coils is related to the eternity of time. Beside him are two groups of six goddesses embodying night's twelve hours.*

RAMESSES

MENPEHTYRE

FIRST CORRIDOR

The tomb of Ramesses I, located in a small lateral valley perpendicular to the main wadi and discovered by Belzoni in October 1817, is of small dimensions but exhibits wall paintings of excellent workmanship strongly reminiscent, from the stylistic point of view, of those in the tomb of his predecessor, Horemheb. Ramesses I (a Greek transliteration of the Egyptian name *Ra-mes-su*), regarded as the first king of the Nineteenth Dynasty and founder of the glorious lineage of the Ramessids, was a soldier and was chosen by Horemheb as successor to the throne of Egypt. The short duration of his reign (less than two years) forced the Deir el-Medina craftsmen to complete his eternal dwelling quickly and accounts for the unusually small dimensions of the corridor and the burial chamber. The tomb is rectilinear in structure

BURIAL CHAMBER

ANNEXE

e f

d

c b a

ANNEXE

ANNEXE

STAIRWAY

FIRST CORRIDOR

STAIRWAY

N

H

G - Ramesses I is welcomed in the Afterlife by Anubis (shown, as usual, in a jackal-headed human shape) and Harsiesis.

H - Overall view of the sepulchral chamber with, at the center, the great sarcophagus of red quartzite. This hall is the only decorated part of the whole tomb, whose small dimensions and the simplicity of its decorative program are explained by the very short reign of

Ramesses I, lasting about sixteen months. Since his tomb is 29 meters long, it is inferred that the workmen prepared the tomb at the incredible speed of 1.8 meters per month.

a - The king facing Ptah and a djed-pillar
b - The king facing Harsiesis and Anubis; Book of Gates
c - Niche featuring a ram-headed deity with Osiris in a chapel and the snake Nesert; Book of Gates
d - The king with the souls of Pe and Nekhen, facing Aten and other deities
e - Book of Gates
f - The king offering wine to Nefertum

and has only one corridor, located between two descending sets of steps, the second of which opens directly into the burial chamber. This is taken up for the most part by a large granite sarcophagus and is flanked by two small annexes. As in the tomb of Horemheb, the scenes and the texts painted on the walls are related to the *Book of Gates*. In the burial chamber, Ramesses, presenting offerings to Atum-Re-Khepri, is led into the presence of Osiris by Horus, Atum and Neith, while in the lateral annex to the left there is a representation of the souls of Pe and Nekhen.

SETHOS I
KV no. 17

Menmaatre
1294-1279 BC

SETHOS MERIENPTAH

MENMAATRE

The tomb of Sethos I, Ramesses II's father, was discovered in October 1817 by the Italian Giovanni Battista Belzoni, a few days after that of Ramesses I. Even though this tomb – still called by the British "Belzoni's Tomb" – was closed to the public in 1991, owing to a real danger of collapse in the burial chamber and in an annex room, its importance is such that we cannot omit its description.

Located in a small lateral wadi in the Valley of the Kings, the tomb of Sethos I is more than 120 meters long and is decorated with colorful paintings and with highly refined bas-reliefs. The structure of the tomb is particularly complex: after a first descending flight of steps, a corridor leads to a second stairway followed by another corridor, opening into a rectangular ritual shaft. Beyond the shaft there

is a room eight meters wide, with four pillars, to which another hall of similar dimensions is attached. From the four-pillar hall a lateral stairway descends to a third corridor and thence to a large six-pillar hall with two small lateral chapels. From the six-pillar hall one finally reaches the burial chamber, whose astronomical ceiling symbolizes the vault of heaven and the main constellations.

In this hall Belzoni found a beautiful empty alabaster sarcophagus, a little less than three meters long, on which were engraved passages from the *Book of Gates*, a text of magical character which relates the journey of Osiris's solar boat through the night's twelve hours, sailing the Underworld river crowded with demons, and lists the magic formulas required to enter the twelve gates guarded by genies and snakes.

This sarcophagus, made of alabaster so thin that it is translucent (it is just five centimeters thick), was brought to England and was subsequently purchased by a British collector,

Sir John Soane, who put it in his London museum-house, in Lincoln's Inn Fields, where it remains today. The mummy of Sethos I was found only in 1881, in the Deir el-Bahri cache.

52-53 Sethos's tomb was discovered by Belzoni on October 18, 1817, a few days after that of Ramesses I. Belzoni, assisted by Alessandro Ricci of Siena, worked for several months in this tomb, carrying out a survey of its wall paintings and drawing this section.

Since at the time the hieroglyphic writing still was a great mystery, Belzoni attributed the tomb to a hypothetical pharaoh called Psammuthis; only later, in 1828, was it identified by Champollion as that of Sethos I.

52 Alabaster statue of Sethos I, son of Ramesses I, the founder of the Nineteenth Dynasty. His reign was characterized by a high artistic level and by a great building fervor, of which the hypostyle hall of Amun's temple at Karnak, the Osireion and the great temple of Abydos and the mortuary temple of Qurna are splendid witnesses. (Cairo Museum)

A - In the four-pillar hall the pharaoh is shown in the presence of diverse deities; in the photograph, Sethos is in the presence of Ptah, the demiurge god of the Memphis theology.

B - The two-pillar hall annexed to the four-pillar hall was called by Belzoni the "Hall of Drawings", since it has remained unfinished. On the walls the ninth, the tenth and the eleventh hour of the Book of Amduat are represented. In the photogaph Sethos can be seen in the presence of Re-Harakhty.

C - On this wall the second and the third hour of the Book of Amduat are illustrated, with the related accompanying texts, describing the journey in the waters of the Afterlife of the solar deity on his boat, escorted by a procession of other boats.

D - Tympanum of the western wall of the burial chamber: Nephthys, at the center of the wall among the royal cartouches, spreads her wings out in à protecting sign.

E - Southwestern corner of the burial chamber with representations of the second and third hour of the Book of Amduat.

F - Detail of the northern heaven in the famous astronomical ceiling of the burial chamber in which are illustrated the main constellations and the heavenly stars. This is the only part of the tomb, apart from the "Hall of Drawings", in which the decorations are not in bas-relief.

G - The boat of Re, shown with a ram's head, accomplishes its night journey in the Underworld.

H - In this little niche Anubis performs the ceremony of the "Opening of the Mouth" in front of Osiris, represented between two imiut-symbols, fetishes of Anubis consisting of an animal's hide attached to a pole placed in a vessel.

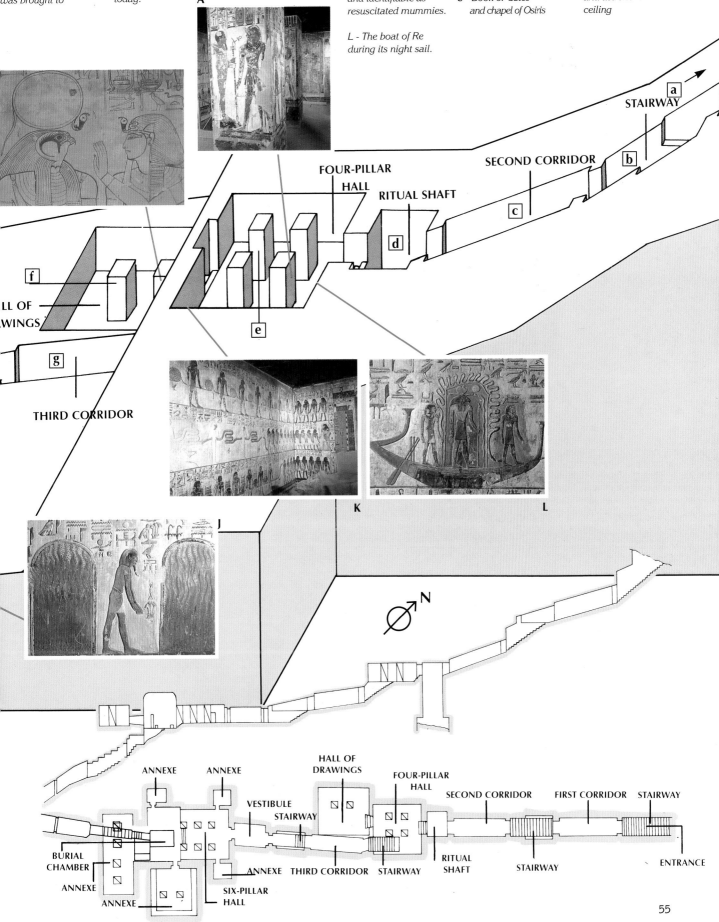

I - The beautiful alabaster sarcophagus on which were delicately engraved passages from the Book of Gates was found by Belzoni in the burial chamber and was brought to London. After having been rejected by the British Museum, it was bought by Sir John Soane, a private collector, and placed in his museum-house, where it remains today.

J - On this side of the tomb the fourth hour of the Book of Gates is described: the genies feed the fire of the "burning wells" into which the damned are to be thrown.

K - On the southeastern side of the four-pillar hall, we find the representation of the Fifth Hour of the Book of Gates: a huge snake crosses several figures dressed in white tunics and identifiable as resuscitated mummies.

L - The boat of Re during its night sail.

a - Litanies of Re
b - Personalities drawn from the Litanies of Re, Book of Amduat, deities
c - Book of Amduat
d - Scenes with deities
e - Book of Gates and chapel of Osiris

f - Book of Amduat
g - "Opening of the Mouth"
h - "Opening of the Mouth"
i - Scenes with deities
j - Book of Gates, Book of Amduat and astronomical ceiling

STAIRWAY

SECOND CORRIDOR

FOUR-PILLAR HALL

RITUAL SHAFT

HALL OF DRAWINGS

THIRD CORRIDOR

N

HALL OF DRAWINGS

ANNEXE

ANNEXE

FOUR-PILLAR HALL

VESTIBULE STAIRWAY

SECOND CORRIDOR

FIRST CORRIDOR

STAIRWAY

BURIAL CHAMBER

ANNEXE

ANNEXE

SIX-PILLAR HALL

ANNEXE

THIRD CORRIDOR

STAIRWAY

RITUAL SHAFT

STAIRWAY

ENTRANCE

C - The sun-god Re, depicted with a ram's head, wanders through the night on his boat pulled by divinities.

B

A

ANNEXE

FIRST CORRIDOR

ENTRANCE

THIRD CORRIDOR

a

b

SECOND CORRIDOR

c

d

e

RITUAL SHAFT

PILLARED HALL

N

F

G

H

F - Wearing a nemes headdress on his head, the pharaoh stands before the Memphite god Ptah. It is interesting to note the numerous graffiti between the two figures, left by visitors who came here in far-off Greek and Roman times.

G - The Litanies of Re are inscribed along the first corridor. The initial part of the text can be seen in this photo: at its center is the disk of the sun, encompassing a kheper-scarab symbolizing the morning sun, and a deity with a ram's head, which personifies the sun at night. The disk puts to flight the enemies all around it (crocodile, serpent and a monstrous creature with horns).

H - This multicolored bas-relief marks the start of the decorative scenes along the first corridor of the tomb. Here the king, wearing an ornate atef-crown, is in the presence of Re-Horakhtis.

a - Litanies of Re
b - Figures taken from the Litanies of Re; Book of Amduat; divinities
c - Book of Amduat
d - Scenes portraying deities

e - Book of the Gates and shrine of Osiris
f - "Opening of the Mouth"
g - Pharaoh with deities and Book of the Dead
h - Book of Gates and astronomical ceiling

TOMBS OF THE TWENTIETH DYNASTY
RAMESSES III
1186 - 1154 BC

KV no. 11

RAMESSES HEQAIUNU

USERMAATRE MERIAMUN

A - Jugs, pots and amphorae are drawn on the walls of this small side room.

B - Representation of the Nile god and of the deities that personified some of the names of Egypt or some cities. Each deity bears a rich offering table and carries on his head the name of the nome that he represents.

The tomb of Ramesses III, known since antiquity, was explored for the first time in modern times by the Scottish traveler James Bruce in 1768, during an adventurous journey which took him all the way to Abyssinia. Bruce named this tomb "Tomb of the Harpists", on account of a marvelous bas-relief representing two blind harpists.

The tomb, decorated with beautiful paintings which have preserved their lively colors, is of imposing dimensions, being 125 meters long, with the typical plan of the Nineteenth Dynasty's royal hypogea, even though it presents some peculiarities both in the decorations and in the internal setting. Off the second corridor, on whose walls are transcribed extracts taken from the *Litanies of Re*, open eight small cells,

arranged in two groups of four on each side, decorated with a series of scenes quite uncommon and interesting, such as the procession of Egypt's protecting deities, the preparation of food, the funerary furniture and the weapons of the king, the food offerings to the god Hapy, embodiment of the Nile as bearer of plenty, and the famous pair of harpists who gave their name to the tomb, singing the praises of the ruler in front of Atum, Shu and Onuris. The representation on the walls of objects and scenes magically assured their eternal existence or accomplishment, at the same time sheltering the deceased from the ravages of ever likelier looting. At the end of this corridor, a little hall marks a sharp change of direction in the axis of the tomb,

C - The pharaoh with the crown of Lower Egypt offers a candle to the god Atum

D - The Memphite demiurgic god Ptah with his composite scepter that combines an ankh-cross, a was-scepter and a djed-pillar, and a rare headdress made up of two curved plumes and a solar disk placed upon his habitual blue or black cap.

E - Belzoni retrieved the lid of the sarcophagus of Ramesses III in 1818. It is conserved at the Fitzwilliam Museum in Cambridge and depicts the pharaoh in relief as Osiris with the atef-crown flanked by Isis and Nephthys. The sarcophagus is in the Louvre Museum.

F - The pharaoh, with a short, blue knitted wig called ibes encircled by a seched-diadem with uraeus, offers incense.

G - The pharaoh, wearing a ceremonial headdress called a kheperesh, offers a torch.

H - One of the two blind harpists behind the name given to the tomb by Bruce in 1768.

I - View of the pillared hall with scenes illustrating the sixth hour of the Book of Gates. In the foreground, on the pillar, Ramesses III is making an offering.

ANNEXE
THIRD CORR.
ANNEXES
VESTIBULE
FOURTH CORRIDOR
RITUAL SHAFT
PILLARED HALL
ANNEXES
BURIAL CHAMBER
ANNEXES

owing to the fact that during the excavation, carried out according to the preestablished plan, the workmen came across the nearby tomb KV no. 10 of Amenemesses (a pharaoh who ruled for a short period of time between Merneptah and Sethos II) and had therefore to change the general direction of the tomb: a case quite unusual but not unique – it also happened in the Valley of the Queens during the building of Nefertari's tomb, where a similar change in the axis is noticed, due to the presence of Tuya's tomb.

The third corridor, off its axis but parallel to the first, is decorated with passages from the *Book of Gates*, in addition to texts from the *Book of Amduat*, and leads to a ritual shaft and, thence, to a four-pillar hall in which, beside Chapters 4 and 5 of the *Book of Gates*, there is a representation of the known human races and scenes of offering to Re-Harakhty, Khepri and Atum, the three forms of the solar godhead.

In the lateral annex, opening off the right side of this hall, there is a scene in which Ramesses III finds himself facing Osiris, who holds out to him a feather, symbolizing the order and justice of Maat. Here ends the part of the tomb open to visitors.

The tomb continues with a fourth corridor leading to a vestibule and, thence, to the eight-pillar burial chamber which sheltered the red quartzite sarcophagus: this was sold to the king of France and is now in the Louvre Museum, while its cover, recovered by Belzoni, was transferred to England and purchased by the Fitzwilliam Museum in Cambridge. The mummy of the king was found in the Deir el-Bahri cache and is now in the Cairo Museum.

Ramesses III, the builder of the temple at Medinet Habu, was the last of Egypt's great pharaohs: during his 32-year reign he succeeded in defending Egypt's borders against external attacks, such as those originating from the Peoples of the Sea in year 8 and from the Libyans in year 11, but his rule ended at an extremely difficult moment from the economic point of view and one of great political uncertainty. With him an entire world, which had experienced transitory crises but also long periods of great splendor, ends forever.

a - Litanies of Re
b - *Personalities drawn from the* Litanies of Re

Left lateral annexes
1 - *The Nile god presenting offerings to deities*
2 - *Procession of the Nile god and of the deities of the nomes*
3 - *The bull and the heavenly cows*
4 - *Harpists facing the deities*

Right lateral annexes
5 - *Osiris on the throne*
6 - *Fields of Iaru*
7 - *Pitchers, pots and vessels*
8 - *Standards, bows and vessels*

c - Book of Amduat
d - *Divine scenes*
e - Book of Gates *and chapel of Osiris*
f - *"Opening of the Mouth"*
g - Book of the Dead *and divine scenes*
h - Book of Gates, *deities, divine scenes and* Book of the Earth

STAIRWAY

ENTRANCE

FIRST CORRIDOR WITH ANNEXES

SECOND CORRIDOR WITH ANNEXES

ANNEXE

BURIAL CHAMBER

VESTIBULE

FOURTH CORRIDOR

PILLARED HALL

RITUAL SHAFT

THIRD CORRIDOR

ANNEXES

ANNEXE

FIRST CORRIDOR

STAIRWAY

SECOND CORRIDOR

ENTRANCE

ANNEXES

ANNEXE

N

RAMESSES VI
1144 - 1136 BC

KV no. 9

RAMESSES AMUN-HER-KHEPSHEF-NETER-HEQAIUNU

NEBMAATRE MERIAMUN

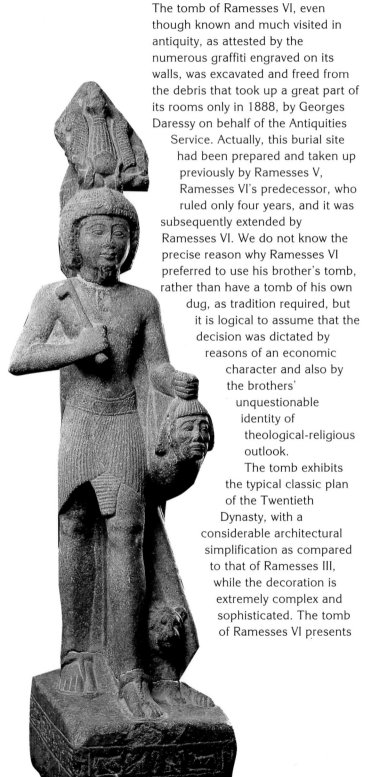

The tomb of Ramesses VI, even though known and much visited in antiquity, as attested by the numerous graffiti engraved on its walls, was excavated and freed from the debris that took up a great part of its rooms only in 1888, by Georges Daressy on behalf of the Antiquities Service. Actually, this burial site had been prepared and taken up previously by Ramesses V, Ramesses VI's predecessor, who ruled only four years, and it was subsequently extended by Ramesses VI. We do not know the precise reason why Ramesses VI preferred to use his brother's tomb, rather than have a tomb of his own dug, as tradition required, but it is logical to assume that the decision was dictated by reasons of an economic character and also by the brothers' unquestionable identity of theological-religious outlook.

The tomb exhibits the typical classic plan of the Twentieth Dynasty, with a considerable architectural simplification as compared to that of Ramesses III, while the decoration is extremely complex and sophisticated. The tomb of Ramesses VI presents

a sort of treatise on theology in which the fundamental elements are the sun and its daily journey in the world of darkness, from which it emerges perpetually victorious, and the light which is its main emanation. The meaning of the wall paintings in the tomb, which have preserved their splendid colors, among which prevail the reds and the yellows, is sometimes obscure and enigmatic in its details. In general, however, it is an analysis of the origins of heaven, of earth, and of the creation of the sun, of the light, and of life.

In the first, second and third corridors, texts from the *Book of Gates* and from the *Book of Caverns*, a collection of texts dealing with Afterlife's sacred geography and with the caverns the sun has to cross during its nightly journey, are painted on the walls. The third corridor ends in a ritual shaft and in a four-pillar hall from which a corridor starts, emerging inside a vestibule: the walls of this entire sector of the tomb continue with the texts of the *Book of Gates* and the *Book of Caverns* begun in the preceding corridors. In the fourth and fifth corridors there are passages from the *Book of Amduat,* and in the vestibule passages from the *Book of the Dead.* The vestibule precedes the burial chamber, where the broken sarcophagus is found: the walls are decorated with the *Book of the Earth*, while on the astronomical ceiling are represented the *Book of the Day* and the *Book of the Night*, illustrated by a double image of Nut in the shape of goddess of the daily and nightly heavens. It is here that the mystery of the creation of the solar disk and of its daily revival took place, in addition to the regeneration of the pharaoh himself, assimilated to the sun.

64 Ramesses VI, represented in this statue as the victor subjugating a Libyan prisoner, succeeded his brother Ramesses V, for whom the tomb KV no. 9 had originally been prepared, in rather unclear circumstances. The story of the reign of Ramesses VI is little known, but his tomb has perhaps the most sophisticated and complete decorative plan of all the tombs of the valley, and its walls constitute a veritable library painted in the rock. The mummy of the pharaoh was discovered in 1898 in the tomb of Amenophis II. (Cairo Museum)

a - Litanies of Re *and*
Book of Caverns
b - Litanies of Re,
Book of the Dead
and Book of the
Caverns
c - Book of Amduat,
*divine scenes and
deities*
d - *Divine scenes*
e - Book of Caverns,
Book of the Earth,
Book of Amduat
and on the ceiling
Book of Day and
Night

The tomb of Ramesses IX, excavated on the left bank of the Valley of the Kings, is the first tomb met by the visitor, after passing through the entrance gate to the site. The tomb is interesting on account of the topics of the wall paintings, taking up again some of the motifs and themes treated in the tomb of Ramesses VI, even if here, on the walls of the first two corridors, the *Book of Gates* is replaced by the *Litanies of Re*, a religious composition celebrating the solar deity in its 75 different transformations during its nightly journey, and its morning resurrection with which the resurrection of the pharaoh himself is identified.

In the second and third corridors, which precede a little rectangular vestibule, there are passages from the *Litanies of Re*, from the *Book of the Dead*, the *Book of Caverns* and, in the last part, from the *Book of Amduat,* with representations of Underworld deities. The corridor and the vestibule are decorated with astronomical ceilings – extremely interesting but not really elaborate in their details. The vestibule leads into inside a four-pillar hall, whence a very short corridor leads to the burial chamber. This has a vaulted ceiling with a double representation of Nut and passages from the *Book of the Day* and the *Book of the Night*, as in the tomb of Ramesses VI.

SECOND CORRIDOR

FIRST
CORRIDOR

ANNEXES

a

ANNEXES

ENTRANCE

A

VESTIBULE

PILLARED
HALL

THIRD
CORRIDOR

SECOND
CORRIDOR

FIRST
CORRIDOR

ANNEXES

ANNEXES

ENTRANCE

BURIAL
CHAMBER

N

THE VALLEY
OF THE QUEENS

The Valley of the Queens is the southernmost of the Theban necropolises. It is where, starting from the Eighteenth Dynasty (about the sixteenth century BC), the first princes and princesses of the royal blood were interred, together with personages living in the court circles and, subsequently, starting from the times of Ramesses II, the queens on whom the title of "Royal Bride" had been bestowed. Later, during the Twentieth Dynasty, Ramesses III renewed the tradition and had the tombs of some of his children prepared in the Valley. The Valley of the Queens, or *Wadi el-Melikat* in Arabic, was so named by Champollion, but originally the Egyptians referred to it as *Ta-set-neferu*, an expression which admits of various interpretations but which can in all likelihood be translated as "the Place of the Children of the Pharaoh", clearly referring to the tombs of the royal princes – rather than "the Site of Beauty", the generally more widespread interpretation. The site was regarded as sacred, and hence suitable for its function of royal necropolis, both for its proximity to the Theban Peak and for the presence at the bottom of the valley of a cave waterfall whose shape and the natural phenomena connected with it could suggest a religious and funerary concept. In fact, the cave would have represented the belly or the womb of the Celestial Cow (one of the figurations of the goddess Hathor) from which gushed out the waters which foretold the impending revival of the deceased buried in this privileged site.

From a typological point of view the burials of the Valley of the Queens can be divided into two large groups: the first includes the funerary shafts (over 60) going back to the Eighteenth Dynasty, the second the large Ramessid tombs of the Nineteenth and

Twentieth Dynasties, which exhibit a complex structure and constitute real funerary apartments modeled on those existing in the nearby Valley of the Kings, of which they would appear to be "simplified versions".

Only starting from the beginning of the Nineteenth Dynasty, with the inhumation of Sat-Re, wife of Ramesses I and mother of Sethos I, did the Valley of the Queens begin to harbour the mortal remains of the royal brides. After the end of the Ramessid period and the subsequent systematic looting of the site by grave robbers, as indicated by numerous juridical papyruses, burials in the valley were resumed: starting from the Twenty-First Dynasty and in the Third Intermediate Period the tombs became a burial site for personages of non-royal blood and essentially employed to the till the soil in the huge estates of the priests.

Turned into a popular cemetery at the beginning of the Roman Empire, the Valley of the Queens kept this status until the mid fourth century AD, when

the Copts settled on the site, burning and irretrievably disfiguring numerous tombs and founding a monastery, Deir Rumi, whose ruins can still be seen today.

Many of the tombs excavated in the Valley of the Queens had suffered in antiquity from serious problems, linked to the hydrogeological and petrographical characteristics of the site. The pharaoh's craftsmen who 3,500 years ago were working to prepare the royal burials in this valley no doubt realized that they had to

work on bad rock. This forced them to make use of peculiar technical devices such as the massive use of *muna*, a special plaster often covering the entire walls and ceilings of the hypogeum. Sometimes the rock was of such poor quality that the ancient architects chose to interrupt the work and start it over again at a new, more suitable, site: this explains the high number of unfinished tombs found in the valley. Also, plentiful signs have been discovered of a period of torrential rains in the post-Ramessid

70 top Overall view of the Valley of the Queens: this was the name given by Champollion to this wide wadi located in the southernmost part of the Theban necropolis, where, starting from the Eighteenth Dynasty, princes and princesses, royal brides and high dignitaries of the court were buried, and which continued to be used as a burial place in the Ptolemaic and the Graeco-Roman age as well.

71 top left
The burial chamber of the tomb of prince Khaemwaset (QV no. 44), one of the sons of Ramesses III, photographed at the moment of its discovery in February 1903. The tomb, used again in a later period, was encumbered with mummies and piled-up sarcophagi.

71 bottom left
One of the members of the Italian Archaeological Mission, headed by Schiaparelli, at work in the tomb of Nefertari (QV no. 66), Ramesses II's "Great Royal Bride", discovered in 1904.

71 right Ernesto Schiaparelli (1856-1928), director of the Egyptian Museum at Turin, headed two excavation campaigns in the Valley of the Queens between 1903 and 1906, with the assistance of Francesco Ballerini, Egyptologist from Como. To Schiaparelli and his team we owe the discovery of the most beautiful and the most important tombs of the valley.

70-71 The Valley of the Queens, called by the ancient Egyptians Ta-set-neferu, a toponym that may be translated as "the Place of the Children of the Pharaoh" or "the Place of the Royal Harem". In the Valley of the Queens there are over one hundred tombs and simple funerary wells.

era, which no doubt had devastating effects on the tombs themselves. The first archaeologist who conducted systematic excavations in the Valley of the Queens was the Italian Ernesto Schiaparelli, director of the Egyptian Museum in Turin, who worked on the spot between 1903 and 1906, assisted by Francesco Ballerini, an Egyptologist from Como. To Schiaparelli's excavations we owe the discovery of all the most important tombs of the site, such as those belonging to the children of Ramesses III, Seth-her-khopshef, Khaemwaset and Amun-her-khepshef. But the most extraordinary discovery was the tomb of Nefertari, Ramesses II's "Great Royal Bride", regarded by many as the most beautiful of all Theban tombs. It was only in 1970 that a series of annual missions began, carried out by the Centre National de la Recherche Scientifique (CNRS) of Paris, the Louvre Museum, and the Centre d'Etudes et Documentation sur l'Ancienne Egypte (CEDAE) of the Egyptian Antiquities Organization. The works made possible the cleaning and a complete survey of the site, in addition to a systematic study of all the burials in the valley, whose original aspect was restored thanks to the removal of backfill materials and of the debris from Schiaparelli's excavations, which had changed the morphology of the valley.

To the Grotto-Waterfall

Ancient Dam

QV no. 86

QV no. 55
Amun-her-khepshef

QV no. 80
Tuya

QV no. 57

QV no. 56

QV no. 54

QV no. 58

QV no. 53
Rameses

QV no. 60
Nebtawy

QV no. 59

QV no. 52
Tyti

QV no. 85

QV no. 62

QV no. 61

QV no. 63

QV no. 51
Isis

QV no. 50

QV no. 49

QV no. 45

QV no. 48

QV no. 47
Ahmose

QV no. 26

QV no. 46
Imhotep

QV no. 44
Khaemwaset

QV no. 40

QV no. 36

QV no. 30
Nebiri

QV

QV no. 34

QV no. 32

QV no. 27

QV no.

QV no. 35

QV no. 37

QV no. 29

QV no. 39

QV no. 43
Seth-her-khopshef

QV no. 38
Satre

QV no. 33
Tanedjem

QV no. 31

QV no. 42
Pa-ra-her-unemef

QV no. 41

Toward the Valley of the Rope

0   10   20   30   40   50 metres

N

Eighteenth Dynasty

Ramesses I - Sethos I

Ramesses II

Twentieth Dynasty

66
tari

QV no. 68
Merytamun

QV no. 71
Bentanta

69

QV no. 73
Henut-tauy

QV no. 74
Duatentopet

QV no. 70

QV no. 72
Neferhat/Baki

QV no. 82

QV no. 75
Henut-mi-re

QV no. 83

QV no. 77

QV no. 79

QV no. 94

QV no. 76

QV no. 78

Entrance Road

Main Wadi

QV no. 20

QV no. 17

QV no. 12

QV no. 11

QV no. 19

QV no. 10

QV no. 8

QV no. 7

QV no. 22

QV no. 18

QV no. 14

QV no. 9

QV no.4

QV no. 5

QV no. 6

QV no. 3

QV no. 2

3

QV no. 16

QV no. 13

QV no. 15

QV no. 81

THE VALLEY OF THE QUEENS

THE TOMBS OF RAMESSES III'S SONS

The tombs of the Valley of the Queens intended for Ramesses III's five sons (Seth-her-khopshef no. 43, Pa-ra-her-unemef no. 42, Khaemwaset no. 44, Ramesses no. 53, Amun-her-khepshef no. 55) are located on the southwestern side of the main wadi and no less than three of them were discovered by the Schiaparelli mission. It is not clear who these princes really were, how old they were, or when and how they died. We know that Ramesses III issued the orders to prepare these tombs in year 28 of his reign, four years before his death. Were the princes therefore already dead at that time, or perhaps were they doomed to die because of an incurable disease? And why were these princes buried in the Valley of the Queens?

74 top This splendid painted bas-relief shows Prince Khaemwaset (QV no. 44) with a typical child's hairstyle: the long hair is collected in a tress, fastened with a braid which falls sideways, covering an ear.

74 bottom On the eastern wall of the antechamber of tomb QV no. 55, Ramesses III introduces his son Amun-her-khepshef, holding a flabellum in his right hand, into the presence of the principal gods of the Afterlife: Ptah, Ptah-Tatenen, Duamutef and Imset.

Perhaps in order to be reconnected with a tradition dating back to the time of the Eighteenth Dynasty? In the nearby temple of Medinet Habu, on the western wall of the second yard, there is a portrait of the royal offspring: thirteen princes and fourteen princesses. Ten of the princes are named – a rather unusual feature, since at that time such representations were generally anonymous. The princes, all bearing the common title of "Standard Bearer to the Right of the King", are distinguished from each other by

their other titles and by their dress. It seems, however, that those lying in the tombs in the Valley of the Queens are not identical with those shown at Medinet Habu.
From a chronological point of view it would follow that the tombs of Seth-her-khopshef and Pa-ra-her-unemef are earlier than Khaemwaset's and Amun-her-khepshef's: these last would appear to have been built in succession, as proved by the complementary sequences of the funerary genies in Chapter 145 of the *Book of the Dead*, which preside over

sumptuously dressed, accomplishes the ritual sacrifices, and it is always he who introduces the sons to the different deities – this being a task normally fulfilled by a god, not by a living ruler. The polychrome bas-reliefs decorating the tomb walls show considerable similarities and comply with a precise decorative plan which expresses belief in a ritual course accomplished by the soul of the prince who descends into the world of the Afterlife, symbolically represented by the tomb. Welcomed by friendly deities, he crosses the doors and the gates of the kingdom of Osiris, watched by different guard genies, who bar whoever does not resort to the magical formulas prescribed in Chapters 145 and 146 of the *Book of the Dead*. Finally the deceased regenerates himself and, by transfiguring himself, "comes out to the light", assimilated to the everlasting stars.

At present the two most beautiful tombs, those of Khaemwaset and Amun-her-khepshef, are open to the public.

the 21 gates of Osiris's dwelling in the Fields of Iaru. The tomb of Seth-her-khopshef never contained the mummy of the prince, who mounted the throne under the name of Ramesses VIII and was buried in the Valley of the Kings.

The tombs of Ramesses III's sons all have a so-called "syringe-shaped" structure: they are essentially a rectilinear corridor with lateral annexes arranged in various ways, leading into the burial chamber, sometimes provided with a small room opening on the rear wall. The tomb of Pa-ra-her-unemef (No. 42) alone substantially differs from this plan, having a far more complex structure with the room of the sarcophagus supported by pillars. It is very similar to the tombs in the Valley of the Kings.

One of the more typical characteristics of the tombs of Ramesses III's sons is that in the decorations the princes are almost always preceded by the king, the real protagonist of the scenes carved on the walls. It is Ramesses III who,

KHAEMWASET
QV no. 44

Eldest son of the king
Sem-*priest of Ptah*
Twentieth Dynasty

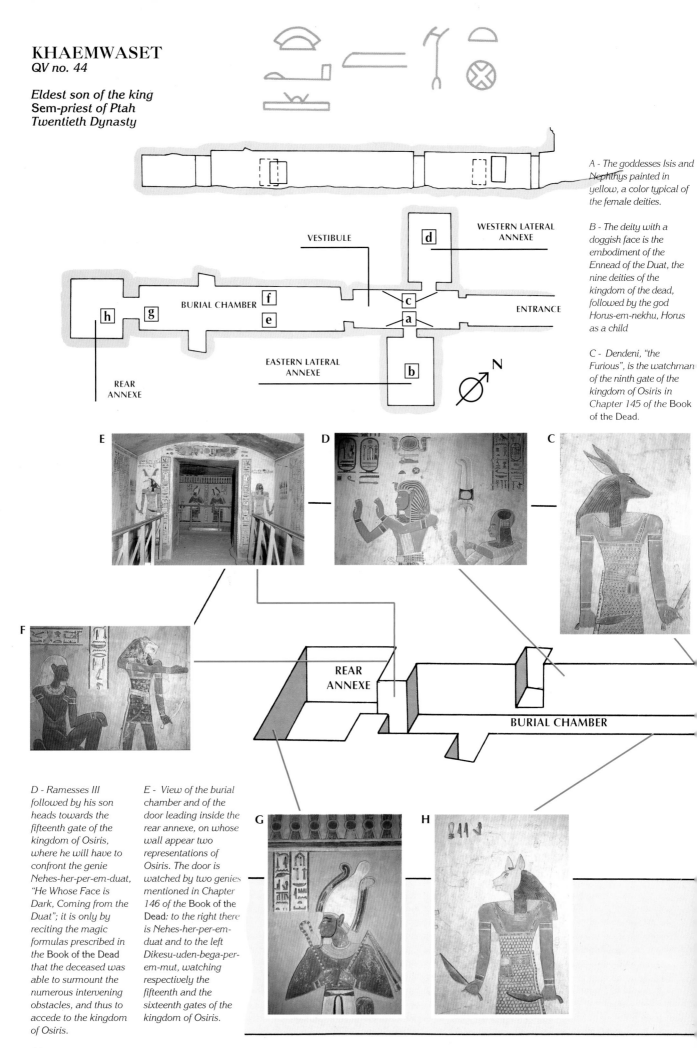

A - *The goddesses Isis and Nephthys painted in yellow, a color typical of the female deities.*

B - *The deity with a doggish face is the embodiment of the Ennead of the Duat, the nine deities of the kingdom of the dead, followed by the god Horus-em-nekhu, Horus as a child*

C - *Dendeni, "the Furious", is the watchman of the ninth gate of the kingdom of Osiris in Chapter 145 of the* Book of the Dead.

VESTIBULE

WESTERN LATERAL ANNEXE

BURIAL CHAMBER

ENTRANCE

EASTERN LATERAL ANNEXE

REAR ANNEXE

N

E

D

C

F

REAR ANNEXE

BURIAL CHAMBER

G

H

D - *Ramesses III followed by his son heads towards the fifteenth gate of the kingdom of Osiris, where he will have to confront the genie Nehes-her-per-em-duat, "He Whose Face is Dark, Coming from the Duat"; it is only by reciting the magic formulas prescribed in the* Book of the Dead *that the deceased was able to surmount the numerous intervening obstacles, and thus to accede to the kingdom of Osiris.*

E - *View of the burial chamber and of the door leading inside the rear annexe, on whose wall appear two representations of Osiris. The door is watched by two genies mentioned in Chapter 146 of the* Book of the Dead: *to the right there is Nehes-her-per-em-duat and to the left Dikesu-uden-bega-per-em-mut, watching respectively the fifteenth and the sixteenth gates of the kingdom of Osiris.*

family having come from the Theban region; but the handle of a box found in her tomb with the ornamental scroll of Pharaoh Ay leads us to surmise a close relation with this king, who was a native of Akhmim, a town sacred to the god Min and located a little over 100 kilometers to the north of Thebes. In the Ramesseum, Ramesses II's imposing funerary temple in Thebes, in the upper part of the second pylon at a height of over ten meters, there is an unusual representation of the Min festival, in which Nefertari dances in front of the sacred bull. Was this a tribute paid to the father of the bride, the pharaoh Ay of Akhmim, Tutankhamun's successor?

Nefertari had five or six sons by Ramesses – some of whom, like the beloved first-born Amun-hi-wenemef, died young – but destiny willed that none of them would mount the throne: Ramesses II had his heir (Prince Merneptah) by another great royal bride, Queen Isis-Nofret, whose tomb has not yet been discovered but is probably located in the necropolis of Saqqara.

The time and the cause of Nefertari's death are unknown to us, but it happened before the celebration of the thirtieth anniversary of Ramesses's reign: the commemorative inscriptions of this period and the subsequent ones no longer carry the name of the beloved wife.

ANTECHAMBER

WESTERN ANNEXE

BURIAL CHAMBER

CELLA

ENTRANCE STAIRWAY

VESTIBULE

SECOND STAIRWAY

FIRST EASTERN ANNEXE

SECOND EASTERN ANNEXE

N

82-83 On the southern wall of the steps leading to the burial chamber, Nefertari stands facing a table of offerings and two braziers, in her customary elegant attire, and performs a wine offering as she holds out two nu-pots to a group of deities (Hathor, Selkis and Maat, not visible in the photograph).
The text in vertical columns says: "The Great Royal Bride, Lady of the Two Lands, She Who Is Rich in Charm, Sweet of Love, Lady of Upper and Lower Egypt, the Nefertari Meri-en-Mut Osiris, Beside Osiris Who Is in the West".

Eastern side of the tomb

A - Nefertari performs offerings to the god Osiris, Lord of the Afterlife, and to Anubis.

B - The goddess Neith welcomes Nefertari.

C - Nefertari is led by Harsiesis in front of Re-Harakhty and Hathor-Imentit.

D - The goddess Isis brings Nefertari in front of the scarab-headed god Khepri.

E - Overall view of the eastern wall of the antechamber and of the vestibule: on the columns we see Osiris to the left and Anubis to the right, while the architrave is decorated with a motif of alternating snakes and ostrich plumes, and at the center there is a genie evoking the eternity of time. Inside we see the god Khepri to the left and Re-Harakhty with Hathor-Imentit to the right.

F - Nefertari with the sekhem-scepter consecrates two large tables of offerings in front of Osiris (to the left) and Atum (to the right), the Heliopolitan creator god considered as a manifestation of Re.

G - Nefertari facing Thoth, the divine scribe, utters the magic formula prescribed in Chapter 94 of the Book of the Dead in order to obtain the scribe's pot and palette of the god together with his magical powers.

N

E

A

D

C

B

I

H - Nefertari makes an offering of linen material to the god Ptah, wrapped up in his classic white mummy-shaped sheath inside a chapel before a djed-pillar. In the texts we read: "To give material to the Lord of the Truth, in the Sacred Land."

I - Nefertari holds out ritual pots containing offerings to Hathor and Selkis while the goddess Maat spreads her wings in a protective attitude.

J - The genies watching the third and fourth gates of the kingdom of Osiris, respectively with heads of crocodile and bull, mentioned in Chapter 146 of the Book of the Dead.

K - Henty-reki, "He Who Drives the Enemy Far Off", watchman of the fifth gate of the kingdom of Osiris.

A - Nefertari playing senet; the royal ba representing Nefertari's soul in the shape of a bird; Nefertari kneeling as she prays.

B - Texts from Chapter 17 of the Book of the Dead. In the upper register, from left: two lions beside the symbol of the akhet-horizon point to Ruty, one of the forms of

Atum, the creator god, father of the god Shu and of the goddess Tefnut; the benu-bird, the ash-colored heron symbol of the soul of the sun-god Re; the goddesses Isis and Nephthys in the shape of falcons protecting the queen's mummy; a deity painted in black with a mystic stick, related to eternity.

C - Corbel with an "Egyptian throat"-style frame, probably meant for the funerary furniture, supported by pillars carrying the royal cartouche.

90-91 The burial chamber seen from the south. On the pillars two forms of Horus are shown related to ancient priestly functions: to the left Horus-iun-mutef ("Horus, Support of his Mother") and to the right Horus-nedj-itef ("Horus Protector of his Father") while in the background can be seen two djed-pillars.

91 bottom On the lower part of the staircase are two large representations of Anubis "the Embalmer, the Great God Who Dwells in the Sacred Earth". In one Anubis is depicted as a black jackal, crouched over a shrine with the nekhakha-flail between his back paws. The god receives Nefertari with a long speech beginning with the words "Come unto me, O worthy consort of the king".

The pillars

The decoration of the pillars in the burial chamber is not only of great interest, but is also perfectly preserved. When entering the hall, the visitor is welcomed by two large figures of divinities wearing leopard skins, that constitute the decoration of the two southern pillars on the southern sides: these are Horus-iun-mutef, that is to say "Horus Support of his Mother" (to the left), and Horus-nedj-itef, "Horus protector of his Father" (to the right) – two forms of Horus linked to ancient priestly functions. On the internal faces of all the pillars, along the longitudinal axis, there are four representations of Osiris "Who Presides over the West, Un-nefer, Lord of the Holy Land, the Great God, the Lord of the Ennead" dressed in the same garment worn by Nefertari: a long white tunic tightened at the waist by a red band tied at the front with two pendants. On the pillars' inner faces, along the transversal axis, there are four large *djed*-pillars, evoking Osiris's spine. These were originally turned toward the sarcophagus, whose main axis coincided with the transversal one of the burial chamber. On the six other sides of the pillars the decorations represent the queen in the presence of diverse divinities: Hathor, Hathor-Imentit, Anubis and Isis.

92 Painted on each of the four inner faces of the pillars is the djed-pillar, which represents the spinal column of Osiris containing the bone-marrow of resurrection. At its side are the scrolls and titles of the queen.

93 top left The god Osiris is portrayed no fewer than four times on the pillars of the sepulchral chamber. Erect inside a shrine, Osiris is shown dressed in the same tunic and red band worn by Nefertari, to indicate that assimilation between queen and god has taken place.

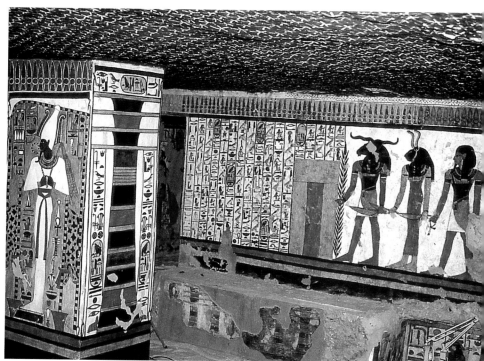

93 top right
The three genies of the second gate of the kingdom of Osiris, referred to in Chapter 144 of the Book of the Dead: Un-hat-sen, Qed-her ("She Who Turns her Head Around") and Imsus.

Each of these genies had a specific role and they are described as "the Doorkeeper", "the Guardian" and "the Annunciator". In the foreground is one of the four pillars, with Osiris and a djed-pillar depicted on it.

93 bottom right
Close-up of the east pillar of the burial chamber, on which Horus-nedj-itef is shown wearing the characteristic leopard skin. Osiris, inside a shrine, can be seen on the other side.

The cella and the lateral annexes

The decoration of the cella is utterly lost today because of the complete detachment of the pictorial layer due to the surface crystalization of salts coming from the underlying rock. The lateral annex opening on the southern side of the western wall has preserved just a small portion of its decoration: among the scenes still visible we see the representation of a building with a façade of pillars evoking Osiris's tomb at Abydos, inside which two of Horus' four sons, Imset and Duamutef, appear between two ibis-headed tutelary spirits, evocation of the Four Winds.
The opposite western lateral annex too is today almost empty, and the only scene still entirely readable shows Nefertari praying in the presence of Anubis and Isis.

The meaning of the tomb

The whole complex decorative program of Nefertari's tomb evokes a ritual journey of the soul of the deceased descending into the subterranean world. This is Osiris's kingdom, symbolized by the sarcophagus hall or "golden hall", to which Nefertari accedes after having crossed the doors and the gates of Chapters 144 and 146 of the *Book of the Dead*. Here take place the gestation and the revival of the queen's soul, which, coming back to the antechamber, is transfigured and shines bright according to Chapter 17 of the *Book of the Dead*, illustrated by the wall decoration of this portion of the tomb. Finally, Nefertari "appears in broad daylight", assimilated to Re rising on the eastern horizon of the sky, following an image evoked on the ceiling of the entrance door of the tomb itself.

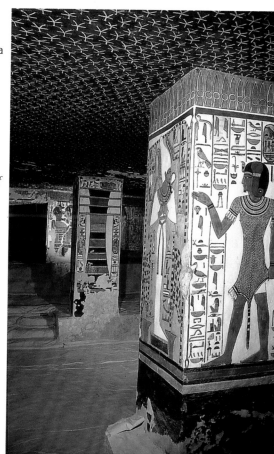

THE TEMPLES OF MILLIONS OF YEARS

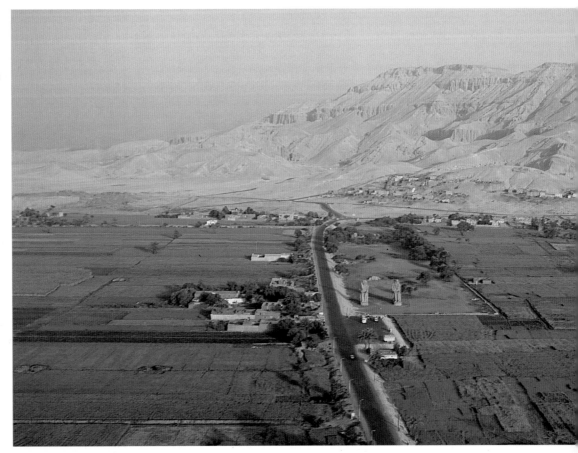

Built on the boundary between the tilled lands which were yearly flooded by the Nile's overflow and the spurs of the Theban mountain, and connected with the river by a network of canals, the temples of the Theban pharaohs of the New Kingdom, lined up parallel to the Nile and roughly oriented in an east-west direction according to the solar axis. These buildings – the majority of which have practically disappeared or survive in such a state as to be hardly interpretable for tourists, like the temples of Amenophis III, Merneptah, Tuthmosis IV, Tuthmosis III and Ramesses IV – were referred to as "funerary temples", but the studies made on the structures and above all on the decorations of the few which are still well-preserved, suggest that they should rather be defined as "temples of the royal worship" or "memorial temples".

In fact, these temples, called by the ancient Egyptians "temples of millions of years", were used for the worship of the king while he was still alive – deified and associated with the worship of the god Amun, principal deity of the Theban pantheon, whose son on earth was the pharaoh. By virtue of this ritual union, taking place yearly on the occasion of the Beautiful Feast of the Valley, the royal power was renewed and strengthened. Also, during the 30th year of the pharaoh's reign the celebration of the *sed*-festival took place in the temples of millions of years.

This was a ceremony of very ancient origin whose aim was to regenerate the king's strength and, through him, that of all Egypt, whose supreme guarantor he was.

VALLEY OF THE QUEENS

TEMPLE OF AY-HOREMHEB

TEMPLE OF RAMESSES III AT MEDINET HABU

COLOSSI OF MEMNON AND THE TEMPLE OF AMENOPHIS III

TEMPLE OF TUTHMOS

94-95 bottom
General view of the necropolis, with the mountain of Thebes behind. Visible in the foreground, behind the two huge statues known as the Colossi of Memnon, is the site where the mortuary temple of Amenophis III once stood.
The funerary temples or temples of royal cult worship, which the ancient Egyptians called "temple of the millions of years" were built on the lower slopes of the mountain. They were connected by a system of canals to the Nile, which reached this level when in flood.

THEBAN
MOUNTAIN

N

NECROPOLIS OF
QURNET MURARI

ANCIENT ROUTE OF THE
WORKERS BETWEEN DEIR EL
MEDINA AND THE VALLEY OF
THE QUEENS

ANCIENT ROUTE OF THE
WORKERS BETWEEN DEIR EL-
MEDINA AND THE VALLEY OF
THE KINGS

VILLAGE ON THE HILL

WORKERS VILLAGE
OF DEIR EL-MEDINA

VALLEY OF THE KINGS

TEMPLE OF
TAWOSRET

NECROPOLIS OF SHEIKH
ABD EL-QURNA

DEIR EL-BAHRI

TEMPLE OF
MERNEPTAH

ANCIENT ROUTE
BETWEEN
DEIR EL-BAH
AND THE VALLEY
OF THE KINGS

NECROPOLIS OF
EL-KHOKHA

TEMPLE OF
THUTMOSIS I

RAMESSEUM

TEMPLE OF
TUTHMOSIS III

NECROPOLIS OF
DRA ABU EL-NAGA

TEMPLE OF
AMENOPHIS
SON OF HAPU

TEMPLE OF
TUTHMOSIS IV

TEMPLE OF
SIPTAH

NECROPOLIS
OF ASSASIF

WESTERN THEBES AT THE TIME OF THE
TWENTIETH DYNASTY WITH EVIDENCE FOR
THE TEMPLES OF MILLIONS OF YEARS

TEMPLE OF
SETHOS I

*95 bottom The
Ramesseum complex
with its adjoining
buildings and the
barely visible remains
of the temples of Siptah
and Tuthmosis III.*

95

96 bottom   The site of Deir el-Bahri, which owes its name to the former presence of a monastery constructed in the Coptic age, is at the bottom of an imposing rock amphitheater at the foot of an impressive cliff. The site, considered sacred to the goddess Hathor, was selected during the Eleventh Dynasty by King Nebhepetre Mentuhotep for the construction of his burial temple. A few centuries later, during the Eighteenth Dynasty, the burial temples of Hatshepsut and Tuthmosis III were built on the same site.

DEIR EL-BAHRI

96-97 The site of Deir el-Bahri is dominated by the grandiose terraced temple of Hatshepsut: at the side can be seen the remains of the two temples constructed by her grandson and successor Tuthmosis III and by the pharaoh Nebhepetre Mentuhotep, founder of the Eleventh Dynasty.

The most famous and the most visited among the temples of Western Thebes is certainly the one Queen Hatshepsut had built at Deir el-Bahri, a valley ending in an ample amphitheater demarcated to the west by the rocky face of the Theban mountain, which separates it from the adjoining Valley of the Kings, to the north by the hill of Dra Abu el-Naga, and to the south by that of Sheikh Abd el-Qurna. The Egyptians held that this valley, anciently called *geser*,

"sacred", was sacred to the goddess Hathor, deity of the multiple attributes, but linked to the funerary worship in the Theban necropolis. At Deir el-Bahri (an Arabic name meaning "Monastery of the North", since in the Coptic era there was a monastery there, now destroyed) no less than three temples were built, arranged alongside each other and belonging respectively to the pharaohs Nebhepetre Mentuhotep, Hatshepsut and Tuthmosis III.

CHAPEL
OF HATHOR

TEMPLE
OF HATSHEPSUT

TEMPLE
OF NEBHEPETRE
MENTUHOTEP

TEMPLE OF
TUTHMOSIS III

THE SITE OF DEIR EL-BAHRI AS IT MUST HAVE BEEN IN THE TIME OF TUTHMOSIS III

N

97

THE TEMPLE OF MENTUHOTEP

King Nebhepetre Mentuhotep was the first to build a temple to the goddess Hathor in the sacred valley. Unlike the other temples of Wester Thebes Mentuhotep's was a real funerary temple where the deceased king – deified and revered together with Amun-Re – was worshipped according to a new theological concept which subsequently spread to the New Kingdom's "temples of millions of years". Mentuhotep, the first ruler of the Eleventh Dynasty, who is credited with the reunification of Egypt, wanted to have a temple built for himself close to his tomb, following a tradition that went back to the Old Kingdom, when the funerary temples were built next to the royal tombs, on the eastern side of the pyramids.

The great architectural novelty of the temple of Mentuhotep is its multi-level layout: a processional road started from the valley temple and led to a vast courtyard shaded by trees arranged in parallel lines. From the yard started a ramp leading

98 This statue of Nebhepetre Mentuhotep in painted sandstone, was discovered at Deir el-Bahri in 1900 by Howard Carter. It was found in the royal cenotaph, under the central mastaba, which is reached through an opening called Bab el-Hosan. The king, who was responsible for the reunification of Egypt after the internal wars that had characterized the First Intermediate Period, is represented in Osiris form with the red crown of Lower Egypt.

A - Courtyard
B - Ramp
C - Terrace
D, E - Ambulatory
F - Mastaba
G - Vestibule
H - Chapels of the tombs of queens and princesses
I - Chapel to Hathor of Tuthmosis III
J - Second courtyard
K - Entrance to the tomb of Nebhepetre Mentuhotep
L - Hypostyle hall
M - Sanctuary carved from rock
N - Niche

BAB EL-HOSAN

through a colonnade to a terrace, in the center of which a mastaba was found. From the yard also opened an underground passage, marked on its surface by a cavity called by the Arabs *Bab el-Hosan*, leading, after 150 meters, to a cenotaph located exactly under the mastaba, where in 1900 Howard Carter, the future discoverer of Tutankhamun's tomb, found a beautiful statue of Mentuhotep in painted sandstone, now kept in the Cairo Museum.

To the west of the terrace and the mastaba a second yard was found, surrounded by pillars and leading to a rocky sanctuary intended for the royal cult and to a complex of six funerary chapels and six tombs intended for the royal brides and princesses. Still in the second yard was found the entrance to another long underground passage, leading to the funerary room dug inside the mountain, according to a concept which eventually found widespread application in the tombs of the Valley of the Kings.

As in the royal necropolises of the Old Kingdom, the funerary complex of Mentuhotep was surrounded by the tombs of princes, princesses and royal brides (from this sector come the magnificent sarcophagi of the royal brides Kawit and Ashait, discovered at the beginning of the century and exhibited at the Cairo Museum), while the leading citizens and the dignitaries had rock tombs built for themselves on the northern side of the valley.

The temple of Mentuhotep, discovered by accident by Lord Dufferin about the middle of the nineteenth century (1859-1869), was subsequently excavated on the initiative of the Egyptian Exploration Society between 1903 and 1907 by Edouard Naville and Charles Currely and, from 1920 to 1931 by Herbert Winlock on behalf of the New York Metropolitan Museum of Art.

The archaeological surveys of the temple were only carried out many years later, between 1968 and 1970 by the German Archaeological Institute at Cairo.

A - Vestibule
B - Hypostyle hall
C - Sanctuary carved
    from rock
D - Vestibule
E - Niche
F - First room
G - Second room

Main scenes:
a - The goddess
     Hathor portrayed
     as a cow
b - Procession of the
     queen's soldiers
     and boats
c - Hathor in the form
     of a cow licks the
     hand of the queen
d - The queen moves
     toward Hathor
e - The queen
     between Amun
     and Hathor
f - Senenmut

THE CHAPEL OF HATHOR

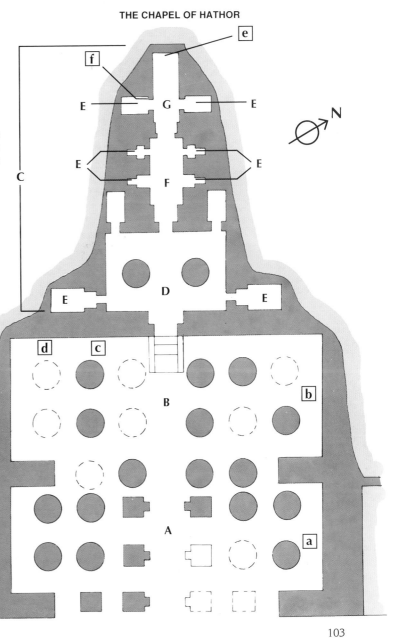

103 top right Bas-relief located in the chapel of Hathor, representing the goddess in the form of a cow with two high plumes that enclose a solar disk.

103 bottom left The entrance door of the rock shrine in the chapel of Hathor.

103

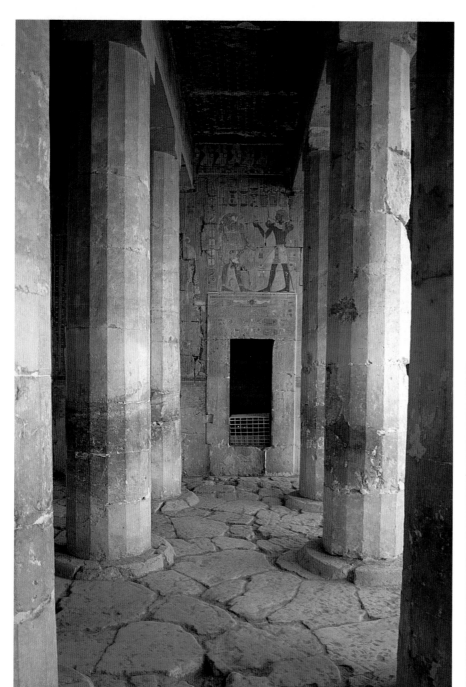

The lower chapel of Anubis

The lower chapel of Anubis has a splendid hypostyle hall with twelve grooved columns and an astronomical ceiling. This is followed by two small rooms at right angles to each other, with vaulted ceilings and farther on there is a niche, also at right angles to the second room.

104 top left
The northern part of the hypostyle hall of the lower chapel of Anubis, is decorated with scenes of offerings to Anubis and to Sokaris.

104 top right
The god Amun with the distinctive attributes of the deity, the was-sceptre and the ankh-cross.

104 bottom The god Thoth, divine scribe.

4 - Men carrying trees

Chests, panthers, etc.

6 - Tributes for the kings of Punt		7 - Hatshepsut offers gifts to Amun	8 - Weighing and measuring	8 -Texts	9 - Official announcement of the expedition's success, before Amun
4 - Ships	5 - The return				
1 - Departure of the fleet					

3 - Presentation of the gifts   Hatshepsut   Heaps of myrrh   Hatshepsut standing   Amun on his throne

2 - Expedition welcomed at Punt. Native dwellings

Three tall trees   Tuthmosis III offers myrrh, in front of the sacred barque carried by priests   10 - Official announcement of the expedition's success, before the court

109 top Key to the interpretation of the "Punt Portico", according to J. H. Breasted (1962).

109 center The Egyptian ships are loaded with products of the land of Punt. The Egyptian expedition had five ships, each about 20 meters long, with a crew of 30 oarsmen.

large quantities of the wonders of the land of Punt, with all the precious woods of the Land of God, heaps of gum of myrrh and living myrrh trees, with ebony wood and pure ivory, with the green gold of Amu, with aromatic wood called *tyshepses* and *khesyt*, with fragrances, incense, antimony, . with baboons, monkeys and dogs, with skins of panthers of the South, with the natives and their sons…"
After showing the return of the expedition to Thebes and the weighing of the imported goods, the bas-reliefs come to an end on the northern part

of the portico by representing the arrival of the god Amun at Deir el-Bahri on the occasion of the Beautiful Feast of the Valley. The queen delivers a long speech to him, stressing the valor of her enterprise that had made it possible to find the way to Punt in order to comply with the god's wish. In his reply, Amun, the Lord of Karnak, praises the queen for all her actions and for the success of the expedition and goes on to say that the precious goods from Punt confirmed he had created that land "to amuse his heart" and that he had provided for the final

109 bottom The precious antyu trees (a word that apparently denotes incense) with their roots, are placed in baskets and carried on board the ships.

success of the difficult expedition so that he could benefit from "all the good and beautiful things from the Land of God", satisfied that Hatshepsut had thus respected his will and honored her divine father. It is known that 31 myrrh trees arrived in Egypt in good condition and were planted in Amun's garden at the temple of Karnak, although different climatic conditions probably prevented them from taking root, which later induced Tuthmosis III and still later Ramesses III to organize new expeditions to Punt.

It is known that ever since the time of the Old Kingdom the Egyptians organized more or less regular expeditions to the land of Punt, primarily with a view to importing incense and myrrh – materials that could not be found elsewhere but were required for celebrating religious cults, in the course of which they were burned in honor of the gods. They also found various uses in the field of medicine, as evidenced by various papyruses, such as Ebers or Harris 716. In particular, myrrh was principally used as a balsam, while incense, besides being burned in special burners for its characteristic

fragrance, was used in combination with other substances, such as honey, myrrh, wax, beer or fruit, for the treatment of numerous disorders from rheumatic pains to stomachache, and from liver disorders to problems of blood circulation and headaches. But where was the mysterious land of Punt? The texts commenting on various depicted scenes give no hint about this. Numerous hypotheses have been advanced, however, and, although there is no reliable proof, it is logical to assume that Punt – which the ancient Egyptians called the "Land of God" – was situated on the shores of the Red Sea. And

indeed, knowing the relatively modest navigational skills of the ancient Egyptians, who were engaged in river navigation much more than in sea voyages, and comparing the average speed of the ships in that age (which amounted to about 3-4 knots) to the time required for completing the

110 left The bas-reliefs show many specimens of the tropical marine fauna typical of the Red Sea, together with freshwater and saltwater fish that would suggest that the land of Punt was located at the mouth of a river.

110 top right The captain of the Egyptian expedition to the land of Punt, followed by his soldiers, offers, according to the hieroglyphic texts, "bread, wine, beer, meat and fruit" from Egypt: how these perishables could have been conserved during the voyage remains a mystery.

110 bottom right The inhabitants of Punt lived in dwellings with conical roofs, built on piles and reached by

ladders. Huts of a fairly similar shape can still be seen today in some regions of eastern Africa.

expedition (about 30 to 40 days for the voyage along the coast using the dominant northerly winds and about three months for the return voyage using oars against the wind), it seems evident that the land of Punt could not lie farther than Cape Guardafui, the southernmost point of the Red Sea. The plants from which myrrh and incense are produced, the *Boswellia* and the *Commiphora*, grow at these latitudes on both the African and the Arabian coasts. Also, the examination of various archaeological objects brought from Punt demonstrates their African origin without the shadow of a doubt. Thus it would be logical to assert that the land of Punt was situated in the area of the Horn of Africa – more precisely, on the coasts of Ethiopia or northern Somalia.

THE BEAUTIFUL FEAST OF THE VALLEY

In the time of Hatshepsut, the chapel of Amun situated on the upper terrace of her temple at Deir el-Bahri was the final destination of the holy procession in the course of the Beautiful Feast of the Valley, which, together with the Festival of Opet, was the main event in the liturgical calendar of Thebes.

The Festival of the Valley, described in the bas-reliefs of the upper terrace, was the most ancient of all the various religious celebrations and took place during the second month of the *shemu* season, that is, during the tenth month of the solar year, which, in the age of the New Kingdom, coincided with the beginning of summer. This recurrent festivity called *pa heb nefer en painet*, or the "Beautiful Feast of the Desert Valley", originated in the time of

Nebhepetre Mentuhotep, and its name is an allusion to the temple that this king had ordered built for himself in a valley situated to the south of Deir el-Bahri and known until this day as Nebhepetre Valley.

The Beautiful Feast of the Valley was, in essence, a "celebration of the dead", in the course of which, as happens today, family members of the deceased visited the tombs of their buried relatives, spent some time there, ate, and received friends who paid their respects. On these occasions, the god Amun,

accompanied by leading inhabitants of Thebes, took part in a large procession on the west bank to visit the gods of the West and the deified dead kings: the priests of the temple of Karnak put a tabernacle containing the holy image of the god on an imitation boat which was carried on the shoulders of the participants up to the jetty, where it was placed on board the magnificent ship *Userhet*, or the "Powerful Prow", which was towed by the king's boat and was followed by the boats of Mut and Khonsu, the other two gods that, together with Amun, formed the Theban Triad. This squadron of boats crossed the Nile and, reaching the west bank, the procession marched toward the temple of millions of years of the king, making its way through the acclaiming crowd of people offering ritual sacrifices of food and bunches of flowers which, on contact with the divine image, became impregnated with the very essence of the deity and were later deposited on the tombs in the necropolis, where they ensured the spiritual revival of the deceased.

The imitation boat of Amun was first carried to the interior of the temple, to its hypostyle hall, then the priests carried the god's tabernacle to a nearby chapel containing also the ritual image of the pharaoh, which magically transformed itself into the sacred image of the god, and left it there for the whole night. On the next day, the procession around the sacred image began anew and included the entire necropolis, making stops in the temples of millions of years of the deceased kings, to guarantee in this way, through assimilation, the eternal nature of this royal cult. The final destination of the procession was the temple of Hatsheput at Deir el-Bahri, in the sacred Valley of Hathor. Here Amun's tabernacle was deposited in the most sacred part of the temple, the chapel of Amun on the upper terrace, where it stayed amid bunches of flowers before it was transported back to Karnak at the end of the celebrations.

111 Transport of the sacred boat of Amun containing the shrine with the image of the god, during the Beautiful Festival of the Valley. On this occasion Amun went *to the western bank and halted in the different temples of the royal worship rendering homage to the deceased deified kings.*

THE CACHE OF DEIR EL-BAHRI

Crossing the mountain range that is the southern limit of the valley of Deir el-Bahri, one would find oneself near a rocky precipice, practically invisible from afar, which originally housed the tomb, made in the form of a shaft, of the royal bride Inhapis (no. 320); it became famous under the name of the "cache of Deir el-Bahri".

In 1881, Gaston Maspero, director of the Egyptian Antiquities Service, alarmed by the appearance on the market of objects originating from the royal tombs, after conducting investigations that led to the identification of a band of robbers operating in the Thebes area and to their confession, found at this site the remains of the most famous Egyptian pharaohs, including those of Ramesses II and his father, Sethos I. In fact the Thebean priests of the Twenty-First Dynasty – around the reign of Pharaoh Siamun (978-959 BC) and of

Chief Priest inudjem II (990-969 BC) – in their attempt to save the royal remains of the most important pharaohs from desecration, which they thought, was becoming ever more probable, since cases of robbery of the royal tombs by expert thieves had occurred already by the end of the Twentieth Dynasty and could become more frequent, decided to hide the remains in this rocky precipice of the mountains of Thebes, which was justly considered more secure than the tombs situated in the Valley of the Kings.

112 top In 1881, Gaston Maspero discovered a hiding-place in a small valley located south-west of Deir el-Bahri, concealed in a bend of the rock wall and practically invisible from a distance. This famous "cache of Deir el-Bahri" contained the mummies of some of the most famous pharaohs of Egypt, transported in secret by priests in order to preserve them from the desecrations that were fairly widespread during the Twenty-First Dynasty.

112 bottom The mummy of Ramesses II was deposited in a wooden sarcophagus reused for the occasion and dating from the late Eighteenth Dynasty. The hieratic text written on the sarcophagus relates the story of the vicissitudes of the mummy which was first transported to the tomb of Sethos I, and then to this last hideout during the reign of Siamon, around 970 BC.

THE SECRET TOMB OF SENENMUT
TT no. 353

**Chief Steward of Amun
Eighteenth Dynasty**

113 top The portrait of Senenmut, the famous architect of Hatshepsut, responsible for construction of her temple at Deir el-Bahri, is portrayed in the astronomical ceiling of his secret tomb (TT no. 353) located northwest of the temple entrance and planned in such a way that the burial chamber is connected with the courtyard of the temple itself.

Just before the entrance to the lower terrace of the temple of Hatshepsut, at the northern side, there is a small but deep hollow opening, remnant of an ancient clay mine, at the end of which is the entrance to the unfinished tomb of Senenmut, the "Chief Steward of Amun", an extraordinary and enigmatic personality who played one of the most important roles during the period of Hatshepsut's co-regency, and primarily from the seventh year of her reign.

Senenmut, who by that time had already had a great and impressive tomb built for himself in the necropolis of Sheikh Abd el-Qurna, near the hill top (TT no. 71), now in a state of complete ruin, later apparently wished to be buried closer to his beloved queen, with whom, certain historians hypothesize, he might have had intimate relations, though they cannot point to any evidence in support of such an assumption. His tomb at Deir el-Bahri was excavated deep into the rock in such a way

that the whole complex was situated in exact correspondence with the first terrace. The long and steep descending corridor enters into a very small room on whose walls there are quotes from the *Book of the Dead*, and which contains the most ancient astronomical ceiling known in Egypt, with the reproduction of the twelve months of the lunar calendar, as well as of the stars and constellations of the northern hemisphere. Starting from there, another descending corridor leads to another room and finally to the burial chamber. By studying the astronomical ceiling it was possible to fix the exact positions of Jupiter and Mars at the time, and by complex mathematical and astronomical calculations to arrive at the year 1463 BC, or year 17 of Hatshepsut's reign. The date and circumstances of Senenmut's death remain a mystery; nor do we know what happened to him after Hatshepsut's death, which occurred in about the 21st year, and the assumption by Tuthmosis III of full powers; nevertheless, it is certain that he fell into disgrace, and his secret tomb was probably abandoned precisely during this period.

113 center and bottom right The tomb's astronomical ceiling contains a very precise representation of the northern constellations and the twelve months of the year, symbolized by circles with radii. By study of the positions of the stars depicted, it has been possible to date this ceiling precisely to 1463 BC, corresponding to year 17 of the reign of Tuthmosis III.

113 bottom Senenmut's secret tomb is a long, narrow corridor descending to a depth of 60 meters and his burial chamber is incomplete. Indeed, Senenmut, who died in disgrace, was buried in another tomb (TT no. 71), which he had prepared for himself in the neighboring hill of Sheikh Abd el-Qurna.

N

FIRST ROOM WITH
ASTRONOMICAL CEILING

SECOND ROOM

BURIAL
CHAMBER

ANNEXE

THE TEMPLE OF SETHOS I

The temple of Sethos I is the northernmost of all the temples of Thebes, near the western border of the village of Qurna. The nineteenth-century travelers called it the "Temple of Qurna" and the local people *Qasr el-Rubaiq*, but the ancient Egyptians called it "Glorious Sethos in the West of Thebes". It is probable that in ancient times the administrative center of Western Thebes was situated there, in the village known as *Heft-her-nebes*, or "City in Front of its Master". Sethos I dedicated this temple to Amun-Re and to the cult of his father, Ramesses I, who, in the course of his brief reign, did not have time to order the construction of his own memorial temple, as is proved by the chapel dedicated to him and situated in the southern part of the temple.

This building, later completed by Ramesses II, included a powerful wall and two pylons made of unburned brick that served as border between the two courtyards. From the great portal of the first pylon, a row of sphinxes crossed the courtyards up to the hypostyle hall. In the southern part of the first courtyard stood a royal palace, built for the first time here but copied repeatedly in the future. Its function was primarily ritual: the royal palace made it possible for the deceased king to materialize during the great festivities in the throne hall, where he was represented by a statue.

Although the pylons of the temple built of unstable materials like unburned bricks have now disappeared completely, the temple itself, constructed of sandstone, is perfectly well preserved. It has a triple structure: in the center is situated the hypostyle hall, decorated with elegant columns in the form of papyrus fascicles, and, as in the temple of Hatshepsut, toward the

114 top View of the remains of buildings adjoining the temple of Sethos I, brought to light by excavations made by the German Archaeological Institute. The ancient name of the temple was "Glorious Sethos in the West of Thebes".

114 center top View of the temple of Sethos I at Qurna, built by "the Road Where Re Sets", as the ancient Egyptians called the roadway which led to the Valley of the Kings. Only the central part of the building, constructed from blocks of stone, is well preserved. Originally in front of it were two pylons made from air-dried bricks, of which few traces remain.

114 center bottom The pharaoh presents offerings to the deified Queen Ahmes Nefertari, wife of Amosis, founder of the Eighteenth Dynasty.

114 bottom Sethos I portrayed as he offers wine in two nu ritual jars.

A - Enclosure wall
B - First pylon
C - Royal palace
D - First court
E - Processional route
F - Present entrance
G - Second pylon
H - Second court
I - Magazines
J - Portico
K - Hypostyle hall
L - Vestibule
M - Sanctuary
N - Room with four pillars
O - Chapel dedicated to the royal cult
P - Court for the solar cult

south there is an area dedicated to the cult of the king, and to the north an area dedicated to the solar cult. The northern sector includes a courtyard with a central altar surrounded by niches housing statues of the king; in this way he could take part in the sacrifices offered to Amun-Re. As for the decorative style, the bas-reliefs adorning the temple walls are extremely elegant and resemble the style typical for the times of the Eighteenth Dynasty. The temple also had warehouses, some of them specially designed for the storage of agricultural products; these structures appeared here for the first time but were developed in the temples built later, particularly in the Ramesseum, the memorial temple of Ramesses II.

Due to its position, the temple of Sethos marked the first stop of the processions organized in the course of the Beautiful Feast of the Valley and continued to perform this function until the Roman era, when the area was transformed into a sort of industrial zone where numerous artisans worked. During the Coptic era, the northern courtyard was transformed into a church, and private dwellings were built within the temple perimeter; also during that period began the process of reusing the more easily transportable architectural elements, which were incorporated into new buildings. The German Archaeological Institute undertook studies and restoration works of the Sethos I temple in 1972, in the course of which some of the structures that had disappeared in the course of time were once again brought to light.

THE RAMESSEUM

The temple of Ramesses II is widely regarded as the most beautiful and elegant monument of Western Thebes. Champollion also held this opinion, and wrote in a letter: "The Ramesseum is perhaps something most noble and pure in Thebes as far as great monuments are concerned." The ancient Egyptians called the Ramesseum the "Temple of Millions of Years of King Usermaatre Setepenre that is Linked to Thebes in the Estate of Amun, West of Thebes"; it was also mentioned by classical writers, such as Diodorus Siculus, who described it in detail under the name of "the Tomb of Osymandias" (this was a corruption of the word *Usermaatre*, the first name of Ramesses II), and Strabo, who referred to it as *Memnonium*. However, it was Champollion who finally gave it the universally accepted name of the Ramesseum.

The construction of the Ramesseum began soon after Ramesses acceded to the throne; it was finished probably some time around the 22nd year of his reign and certainly before the 30th year, when the great royal jubilee celebrations, or the *sed*-feast took place. The Ramesseum occupies an area of about 15,000 square meters, and is a structure of a classical type reproducing the fundamental motifs of the temple of Sethos I: an external belt, two pylons, and two courtyards which precede the complex of the hypostyle hall, situated at a higher level relative to the plane of the courtyards. However, the architects, Penre and Amenemonet, introduced various architectural and stylistic innovations, such as the use of sandstone for the pylons and the construction of dromoi flanked by sphinxes in parallel to the three sides of the exterior belt. Outside the central structure of the temple there are other structures, represented

A - First pylon
B - First courtyard
C - Royal palace
D - Colossal statue of Ramesses, "Sun of Princes", originally flanked by the statue of his mother, Tuya
E - Second pylon
F - Second courtyard
G - Original position of the colossal statue of Ramesses II (the head was carried off to London by Belzoni)
H - Vestibule
I - Hypostyle hall
J - The "Hall of the barks" with its astronomical ceiling
K - The "Hall of the Litanies"
L - Sanctuary
M - Temple of Tuya and Nefertari

Description of the scenes:
a - Battle of Qadesh
b - Seige of the Syrian city in year 8 of the reign
c - Battle of Qadesh and Festival of Min
d - Seige and capture of the cities of Dapur and Tunip

e - Ramesses II is consecrated and crowned by Sekhmet, Amun-Re and Khonsu
f - Barks during the procession of the Beautiful Feast of the Valley
g - Litanies to Re-Harakhty and to Ptah

116 top Hieroglyphs stating the name used in ancient times for the Ramesseum. The transcription reads: "Temple of Usermaatre Setepenre that is Linked to Thebes in the Estate of Amun to the West of Thebes".

117 right The ancient name of the Ramesseum is inscribed on a block of stone.

principally by large warehouses of unburned brick with vaulted ceilings, situated to the north, west and south of the complex and intended for the storage of various products from the numerous possessions of the temple. These served both for the daily ritual sacrifices and as subsistence for the priests who conducted the services at the temple. In addition, a temple dedicated to Tuya, mother of Ramesses II, and to his wife, Nefertari, was built alongside the northern wall of the hypostyle hall, while near the north-western corner of the exterior belt there was a chapel dedicated to Princess Meritamun, and along the southern belt a chapel dedicated to Prince Wadjmes, son of Tuthmosis I, that was built during the time of Ramesses.

116-117 General view of the entire Ramesseum complex. Early in the twentieth century the Ramesseum was surrounded on three sides by embankments. Until the construction of the Aswan Dam, when the Nile was in flood its waters reached the foot of the first pylon, on the edge of what are now cultivated fields.

118 top A relief (originally colored) depicting the battle of Qadesh.

118-119 View of the second courtyard and second pylon of the Ramesseum, with the colossus of Ramesses II, "Sun of Princes", lying on the ground.

118 bottom left An aerial view of the second court, vestibule and hypostyle hall of the Ramesseum. At the top of the photo it is possible to make out the foundations of the temple of Tuya.

118 bottom right The gigantic feet and other fragments of the colossus of Ramesses, "Re of Rulers", now lying on the ground in the first court

The first pylon, a greater part of whose northern tower collapsed due to ground subsidence, was decorated with war scenes, some of which depicted the famous battle of Qadesh fought by the king against the Hittites near the Orontes river in Syria during the fifth year of his reign. Crossing its monumental threshold, now temporarily obstructed by a mass of unburned brick supporting it to prevent collapse pending restoration, one enters the first courtyard, in whose southern part the royal palace once stood.

On the northern and southern sides of the first courtyard there were two porticos, while on the western side stood a colossal statue of the king, side by side with that of his mother, Tuya. This gigantic granite statue, which was originally some 20 meters high and represented Ramesses as the "Re of Rulers", is now lying on the ground face down, probably because the excavation of blocks of rock from its base disturbed its balance.

This gigantic image of Ramesses II

119 top left Detail of the relief showing the capture of Dapur.

119 top
Transportation of the barks of the deities during the Beautiful Feast of the Valley.

119 center The first pylon seen from the first courtyard. The monumental gateway has been temporarily supported with air-dried bricks to increase its structural stability. Subsidence has already caused serious damage, in particular the collapse of part of the north tower.

119 bottom
A statue of Merit-Amun, also known as the White Queen, daughter and great royal bride of Ramesses II. The statue previously stood in the northwest sector of the Ramesseum, where there was a shrine dedicated to the queen.
(Cairo Museum)

inspired the English poet Shelley, who wrote the following lines:
"My name is Ozymandias, king of kings:
Look on my works, ye Mighty, and despair!"
The second pylon, of which only the northern tower remains, opened the way to the second courtyard, situated at a higher level that could be reached by the front staircase. This courtyard, which now houses the visitors' entrance, was completely surrounded by a portico whose eastern and western sides were decorated with gigantic statues often referred to as the "Osirian colossi" and representing Ramesses in the form of a mummy,

his arms crossed, holding a flail (nekhakha) and a scepter (heqa), the characteristic attributes of Osiris. On the western side of the second pylon, a large colored bas-relief continues the theme of the battle of Qadesh depicted on the first pylon; descriptions of episodes in connection with the king's military activities in the Near East during the eighth year of his reign can be found on both sides of the bas-relief, while the upper parts illustrate episodes in connection with celebrations of the first harvest devoted to the god Min, with scenes of birds being set free to the four corners of the universe, and the dance of Nefertari.

120 top left View of the west part of the Ramesseum and the "Hall of the Litanies", with the Sanctuary.

120-121
The head of the young Memnon is transported from the Ramesseum to the Nile, in a watercolor by G. B. Belzoni, who himself organized this feat in November 1816.

120 bottom left The bust of the colossal statue of Ramesses II, called by Belzoni "Young Memnon", currently on display at the British Museum.

120 bottom right The lower part of the colossal statue of Ramesses II that stood on the left of the main stairway leading to the hypostyle room is still in place; the bust is currently on display in the British Museum.

Three front staircases led from the second courtyard to the vestibule. The central staircase was flanked by two granite colossi representing the king, of which now remain only the very beautiful face of the northern statue and the pedestal of the southern one, whose upper part, which was lying on the ground, evidently as a result of the earthquake that occurred in the second half of the eighteenth century,

was taken to England in 1816 by Belzoni and is now exhibited in the British Museum. A triple door led from the vestibule to the hypostyle hall, whose eastern side was bordered by a wall of which only the southern part is visible now. The hypostyle hall, supported by 48 extremely elegant columns in the form of papyrus fascicles, was decorated with bas-

reliefs representing, in their eastern part, episodes of the military activities of the king in the Orient, such as the capture of the city of Dapur (the southeastern wall) in the eighth year of his reign, or the king's relatives, such as his mother, Tuya, his royal bride, Nefertari, and the royal princes and princesses (the northeastern wall). The western part of the hypostyle, on the other hand, shows episodes from various royal functions, such as the bestowal of the crown by the goddess Sekhmet, on either side of whom Amun-Re and Khonsu can be seen (the northwestern wall), or the bestowal of the scepter, symbol of royal power, by Amun accompanied by Mut (the southwestern wall).
A large door leads from the western part of the hypostyle to a small room called the "Astronomical Hall" or the "Hall of the Barks", decorated with bas-reliefs illustrating episodes of the Beautiful Feast of the Valley, such as boarding the boats participating in the river procession that began at Karnak; this room of the temple supported by eight columns is famous for its splendid astronomical

ceiling, a sort of celestial calendar where the constellations and the 36 Decans are clearly visible. It evidently served to determine the exact timing of religious functions and liturgical celebrations. The "Astronomical Hall" is followed by the "Hall of the Litanies", which has the same eight-column architectural structure; its bas-reliefs show Ramesses in the act of offering sacrifices as well as sacrificial libation and burned offerings to Re-Harakhty (the southeastern part) and to Ptah (the northeastern part).

Abandoned toward the end of the Twentieth Dynasty, the Ramesseum was used as a burial ground for the priests of Thebes in the course of the Third Intermediate Period and as a quarry for building materials during the Twenty-Ninth Dynasty, when, under Pharaoh Achoris, the temple of Tuya and Nefertari was demolished with a view to reusing the blocks in Medinet Habu, and was finally transformed into a church by the Coptic communities who settled in Western Thebes in the fourth century AD.

121 top The stores of the Ramesseum were housed in large vaulted buildings made from air-dried bricks.

121 center The granite head of one of the two colossal statues of Ramesses II that flank the main stairs leading to the hypostyle room.

121 bottom The dedicatory inscription with the royal cartouche, carved later on the bottom part of the statue of Ramesses II, left on the site: here Belzoni inscribed his name and the date of his achievement.

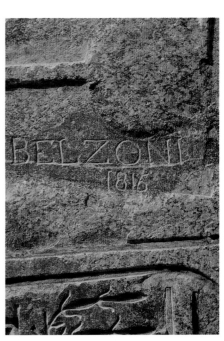

THE COLOSSI OF MEMNON

These two enormous monolithic statues stood on each side of the monumental door of the first pylon of the memorial temple of Amenophis III, now completely destroyed, but thought to be the biggest of all Theban temples. This temple, built on the farther side of the Nile's fluvial plain, was destroyed by annual floods and used as a quarry for extracting building materials. The two colossi, representing the deified pharaoh, serve as the most vivid testimony of that grandiose construction: the statues, 16.6 meters high, are cut from two blocks of quartzite from the quarry of Gebel el-Ahmar near Cairo. As a result of an earthquake in 27 BC, as recorded by Strabo (see Strabo, *Geography*, XVII, 1, 46), the northern colossus partly collapsed. After that, an extraordinary phenomenon took place in the morning: due to heating by the sun's rays and to the humidity of the night, the statue emitted sounds that, according to Pausanias, resembled those of a zither.

The ancient Greeks looked for an explanation in the legendary story by Homer about Memnon, the son of Eos (Aurora) and Titon, who was killed by Achilles and reappeared in Thebes as a statue, and every morning lamented at the sight of his mother rising in the skies. This phenomenon, which acquired great fame in ancient times and attracted numerous visitors from every corner of the region (confirmed by numerous Greek and Roman signatures and inscriptions cut on the pedestal and on the feet of the statue), ceased after the restoration works ordered by Emperor Septimius Severus at the end of the second century AD.

122 top left Detail of the top part of the northern colossus: this was the statue which in the early morning, in ancient times, emitted a curious lament-like note.

122 bottom left The southern colossus. Each of the two statues was hewn from a single block of stone and rested on a base. Altogether they stood about 16.6 meters high.

122-123 The Colossi of Memnon stood in front of the first pylon of the great mortuary temple of Amenophis III, now destroyed. The two colossi were flanked by two smaller statues of the royal wife, Teye, and the mother of Amenophis III, Mulemula.

122 bottom Detail of the southern colossus: Queen Teye, wife of Amenophis III, is portrayed - as was customary - on a small scale, beside the leg of the king.

*123 top On the back
side of each statue is
a column with a
dedicatory inscription.*

*123 center
Aerial view of the
Colossi of Memnon
and the area beyond,
where the temple of
Amenophis III, the
largest of all the
Theban temples, once
stood.*

*123 bottom Plan of
the temple of
Amenophis III,
designed by the
celebrated architect
Amenhotep, son of
Hapu (according to
Haeny).*

A - *Colossi of
     Memnon*
B - *Enclosure wall*
C - *First pylon*
D - *Second pylon*
E - *Third pylon*
F - *Solar court*

N

E

D

C

B

A

**THE TEMPLE OF AMENOPHIS III
AND THE COLOSSI OF MENNON**

MEDINET HABU

Medinet Habu, a small village situated a little over two kilometers to the south of the Ramesseum, was called *Djanet* by the ancient Egyptians and, according to popular belief, it was the place where Amun appeared for the first time. This is why, from ancient times, it was the place of worship dedicated to this god, as evidenced by the existence here of a temple of the Eighteenth Dynasty dedicated to Amun of Djanet, built during the time of Hatshepsut and Tuthmosis III, probably on the ruins of a still more ancient temple. This is what later induced Ramesses III to order the construction there of his own memorial temple. The name Medinet Habu – or "the City of Habu" – as the village is now called in Arabic, is of uncertain origin. According to one hypothesis, *habu* is connected with the word *hbw* which means ibis, the

**THE MEDINET
HABU COMPLEX**

A - Entrance
B - Migdol
C - Chapel of the
    Divine Adoratrices
D - Temple of the
    Eighteenth
    Dynasty
E - Temple of
    Ramesses III
F - Royal palace
G - Magazines
H - Sacred lake
I - Nilometer

124 top Aerial view of the site of Medinet Habu, surrounded by a massive wall made from air-dried bricks. Dominating the site is the huge temple of Ramesses III, flanked by the smaller temple of the Eighteenth Dynasty. Just visible to the right are the ruins of the mortuary temple of Ay and Horemheb, now totally destroyed.

124-125 The court and gigantic first pylon (with a length of 63 meters and average height of about 20 meters) of the mortuary temple of Ramesses III. Its general plan was modeled on that of the Ramesseum, of which it can be considered a larger version.

124 bottom left Hieroglyphs giving the name used in ancient times for the temple of Ramesses III. The transcription reads: "Temple of Usermaatre Meriamun that is Linked to Thebes in the Estate of Amun, West of Thebes".

124 bottom right The temple of Ramesses III differs from other mortuary temples: standing before it is a fortified migdol tower, built along the same lines as Oriental fortresses

N

sacred bird of Thoth, because nearby, in Qasr el-Aguz, there was a small Ptolemaic temple dedicated to Thoth. It is also possible that the word *habu* is derived from Hapu, since the funeral temple of Amenophis, son of Hapu, the famous architect of Amenophis III, exists in the immediate vicinity. In the first millenium BC, Djanet was also thought to be the burial place of the Ogoad, the first four divine couples. At certain regular times – the so-called "Feast of the Tenth Day" – the creator-god Amun-em-ipet ("Amun is in his Harem") travelled to Djanet from his residence in the temple of Luxor, the birthplace of the gods that comprised the Ogoad, to re-perform funeral rites for his ancestors, thereby giving them new life and thus renewing creation.

ARTIST'S IMPRESSION OF THE TEMPLE OF RAMESSES III

A - First pylon
B - First courtyard
C - Window of the Appearances
D - Bell-shaped columns
E - Osirian pillars
F - Second pylon
G - Portico with Osirian pillars
H - Second courtyard
I - Ramp
J - Portico with Osirian pillars
K - Large hypostyle room
L - Royal treasure rooms

M - Chapels dedicated to various deities and to the deified Ramesses
N - Second hypostyle room
O - Third hypostyle room
P - Chapel of Ramesses III
Q - Chapel of Re-Harmakhis
R - Shrine of the sacred bark of Amun
S - Chapels of Mut and Khonsu

Main scenes
a - Hunting the wild bull
b - Religious calendar; text of year 12
c - Ramesses's expedition in Upper Egypt
d - Naval battle against the Peoples of the Sea
e - The king with prisoners and Philistines
f - Libyan wars
g - Destruction of the Hittite strongholds
h - The pharaoh carries out the ritual sacrifice of the prisoners before

Re-Harakhty and Amun-Re
i - The pharaoh carries out the ritual sacrifice of the prisoners before Amun-Re and Ptah
j - The pharaoh defeats the Libyans; text of year 2
k - The king goes to the Beautiful Feast of the Valley; military parade
l - Fight scenes and equestrian scenes.
m - The king sacrifices the prisoners to Amun and Mut
n - Upper register - the

king makes an offering to various deities; lower register - battle scenes
o - Triumph of the pharaoh and parade of prisoners
p - Feast of Sokar
q - Counting of the hands and phalluses cut from the enemy
r - Upper register - the king makes an offering to various deities; lower register - representation of the sons of Ramesses III

s - Upper register - Feast of Min; lower register - procession of the barks of Amun, Mut and Khonsu
t - The king before a deity
u - Ramesses III makes offerings to Amun and presents the treasure.

| Column | ◎ |
| Osirian pillar | ⊐ |

During the Twentieth Dynasty, Djanet became the administrative center of Western Thebes and the meeting-place of the striking workers and artisans of Deir el-Medina, who stayed there waiting for their demands to be accepted. Later, by the end of the Twentieth Dynasty, this site became a place of refuge for the population during the war waged by the high priest of Amun of Karnak against the viceroy of Kush, and still later, in the period of the Twenty-Fifth and Twenty-Sixth Dynasties, it was the place where the cult of the Divine Adoratrices of Amun was celebrated. The Medinet Habu complex was expanded during the

can hardly equal the elegance of its forms and the balance of dimensions. A unique feature of this temple, that used to be called in ancient times "the Temple of Usermaatre Meriamun Who Joins Eternity in the Estate of Amun in the West of Thebes", is the presence on its eastern side, in front of the first pylon, of a tower built in the form of a *migdol* (a military fortress in Asia Minor). This gave the temple the aspect of a fortress and had protective functions in the large wall surrounding the temple. On passing through the *migdol*, one enters a vast space preceding the first pylon where, to the left, one can see the

process of ritual massacre of Asian prisoners in front of Amun-Re (the southern tower) and of Nubian and Libyan prisoners in front of Amun-Re-Harakhty (the northern tower). On the southwestern side of the pylon is a brilliantly illustrated scene of bull-hunting in the marshes; it is considered one of the artistic masterpieces of the Twentieth Dynasty. Having passed through the gigantic opening of the first pylon, one enters the first courtyard, on whose northern and southern sides are two porticos; the southern portico has an opening, the so-called "Window of Appearances", connected to the royal palace situated outside. The dominant theme of the bas-reliefs in the first courtyard is the annihilation by the king's troops of the enemy (the Libyans and the Peoples of the Sea) whom Ramesses fought during the eighth year of his reign. On the walls are shown not only the vanquished enemies – who can be recognized by an exhibition of

Greco-Roman period, and its long history still continued between the first and ninth centuries AD, when the Coptic city of Jeme was built in the area and a church was constructed in the second courtyard of the temple. The excavations of Medinet Habu began in 1859 and, since 1924, studies at the site have been carried out by the Oriental Institute of the University of Chicago, which has published the complete epigraphical and architectural documentation of the temple.

The temple of Ramesses III

The temple of Ramesses III is the best preserved among all temples of Thebes, and its decorated surfaces amount to 7,000 square meters. The structure of the temple and its iconographic system are similar to those of the Ramesseum, although it

funeral chapels of the Divine Adoratrices of Amun and, to the right, the temple of Amun of the Eighteenth Dynasty. The external lateral walls of the temple are covered with important bas-reliefs; of particular interest among them are those of the northern wall illustrating the battles fought by Ramesses III against the Peoples of the Sea. On the southern wall, numerous liturgical festivities are listed and reproduced, as well as the economic resources of the temple necessary for its complex functioning and brought there from the numerous possessions donated to the temple by the king at the time of its inauguration. The first pylon, on which one can see four large hollows intended to hold wooden poles from which flew the divine insignia, is decorated with bas-reliefs showing Ramesses III in the

126 left This splendid relief, on the southeast part of the first pylon, shows the pharaoh on his war-chariot as he chases a wild bull in the marshes, followed by a procession of young princes. Thanks to its exceptional sense of movement, force of expression and general elegance, this work of art is considered one of

the masterpieces of the Twentieth Dynasty.

126 top right On the north and south sides of the first courtyard is a portico supported by square columns with Osirian pillars; delimiting the west side is the second pylon, through which the second courtyard is reached.

126 bottom right
A relief on the left post of the opening of the second pylon portrays the Peoples of the Sea – in particular Philistines with their distinctive headdresses.

127 top *From the second courtyard a wide ramp gives access to the portico, embellished with Osirian colossi, and from there to the hypostyle halls.*

courtyard (the eastern part of the southern portico), but, farther on, there are illustrations of great religious festivities dedicated to Sokar-Osiris (southern portico) and to Min (northern portico). The wall of the western portico, from which a staircase leads to the first hypostyle hall, is dedicated to the theme of royal power: in the northern part the king is being purified by Thoth and Horus, and in the southern part one can see a scene representing the pharaoh's accession to the throne, where he is accompanied by Thoth in front of the Theban Triad. This wall also features the pictures of the sons of Ramesses III, the future Ramesses

divinities. Moving toward the west, one enters the second hypostyle hall, supported by eight columns, with two groups of lateral halls annexed: those in the southern part were dedicated to the Osiris cult of the deified king, while those in the north were dedicated to various solar gods, among whom the dominant role belonged to Re-Harakhty, with whom the king was identified in his celestial resurrection. Then follows the third hypostyle hall, whose structure is identical to the previous one and whose lateral chapels are dedicated to various gods: Horus and Mut in the south, Amun-Re, the Ennead of Heliopolis, Min, Mut, and Khonsu in the north.

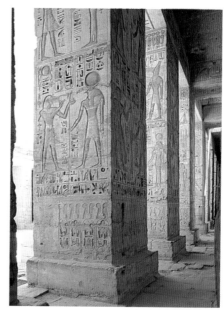

parts of their bodies – but also the war booty, duly listed and quantified, together with the hands and sometimes the phalluses which the pharaoh's soldiers used to cut off the dead bodies of the vanquished enemies to show their own valor. The first courtyard is closed on the north by the second pylon, whose door leads to the second courtyard. The second courtyard, which was also referred to as the "Courtyard of the Feasts", is surrounded by a peristyle: both porticos on the eastern and western sides are decorated with eight Osirian columns, while those to the north and south are supported by large columns in the form of papyrus scrolls. At first, the decoration motifs continue the military themes characteristic of the preceding

IV, VI, VII, and VIII, whose images were added in succession as these princes acceded to the throne. The first hypostyle hall, of which only the base of the 24 columns that supported the ceiling now remain, has in its southwestern part a complex of four rooms, evidently intended to serve as treasury for the temple, as is proved by bas-reliefs on the walls representing heaps of gold, silver and precious stones. Two more annexes situated in the corner between the first and the second hypostyle halls were intended to serve as sites for the cult of the god Montu (the first) and as an additional treasury (the second). The northern side of the hypostyle hall contained a group of five contiguous halls, perpendicular to the axis of the temple and dedicated to various

127 center left *On the north side of the second courtyard bas-reliefs depict the procession of sacred barks.*

127 bottom *General view of the hypostyle halls, of which only the bases of the columns remain.*

127 center right *The square columns of the second courtyard are decorated with scenes which show the pharaoh presenting offerings to the deities.*

The royal palace

In the southern part of the temple grounds, within the space between the first and the second pylons, one can clearly see the foundation of the royal palace. This was built in two stages and was directly connected with the first courtyard of the temple via the "Window of Appearances", through which the pharaoh made his public appearances. However, it is not known for certain whether the royal palace was in fact only a symbolic and ritual construction or whether it was indeed used by the pharaoh when he traveled to the western bank to preside over the most important religious ceremonies.

The chapels of the Divine Adoratrices of Amun

The funeral chapels of the Divine Adoratrices of Amun are situated in a small building in the southeastern part of the space in front of the first pylon. In the course of the Intermediate Period and in the period of the Twenty-Fifth and Twenty-Sixth Dynasties (eighth and seventh

128 top Like the Ramesseum and the temple of Sethos I, the temple of Ramesses III also had an adjoining royal palace where the pharaoh may have resided during important religious festivities.

128 center The royal palace communicated with the temple via a window in the south side of the first court: the pharaoh made public appearances from this window.

centuries BC), certain Divine Adoratrices of Amun were worshiped. These were royal princesses and priestesses enjoying great prestige and representing the pharaoh in the territory of Thebes, such as Amenirdis, the sister of King Shabaqo, Shepenwepet, the daughter of Osorkon III, and Nitocris, the daughter of Psammetichus I – all of them buried within the Ramesseum.

128 bottom During the excavation of the royal palace these colored faience tiles came to light. They show prisoners from different countries and relate to the king's military campaigns: from the left, a Libyan, a Nubian, a Syrian, a Shasu Bedouin from Syria and a Hittite. (Cairo Museum)

A - Chapel of Amenirdis
B - Chapel of Nitocris
C - Chapel of Shepenut
D - Chapel of Mehetnusekhet

THE CHAPELS OF THE DIVINE ADORATRICES OF AMUN

The Temple of the Eighteenth Dynasty

To the north of the principal temple of Ramesses III stands the temple of the Eighteenth Dynasty dedicated to Amun by Hatshepsut and Tuthmosis III. This original building was repeatedly enlarged and modified up to the Ptolemaic and Roman periods. Numerous decorated blocks which originated from the temple of Tuya and Nefertari, adjacent to the Ramesseum, were added to the building in the course of the Twenty-Ninth Dynasty, during the reign of Achoris; the eastern pylon, however, was added in the Ptolemaic period, while the courtyard and the structures preceding it were included during the Roman period. Directly to the north of the temple there are the remnants of the sacred lake, a symbolic representation of the primordial waters, and further to the west, a Nilometer.

THE TEMPLE OF THE EIGHTEENTH DYNASTY

A - Roman courtyard
B - Roman portico
C - Ptolemaic pylon
D - Colonnade of Nectanebo
E - Pylon of Shabago
F - Courtyard with columns
G - Peristyle
H - Chapel of Hatshepsut and Tuthmosis III
I - Chapel
I' - Naos in pink granite
J - Shrine
K - Room of Achoris
L - Door of Nectanebo
M - Door of Taharqa
N - Sacred lake

129 left View of the enclosure wall of the Medinet Habu temple with the two towers of the migdol and the Ptolemaic pylon of the small temple of the Eighteenth Dynasty.

129 right The small temple of the Eighteenth Dynasty, situated to the east of the first pylon of the temple of Ramesses III, was dedicated to the god Amun. In the Ptolemaic period it was enlarged with the addition of a pylon.

THE WORKERS' VILLAGE OF DEIR EL-MEDINA

The site of Deir el-Medina lies in a small valley between the western slope of the Theban mountain and the small hill of Qurnet Murai, not far from the Valley of the Queens, barely a kilometer to the south, and from the Valley of the Kings on the opposite side of the mountain. The name of Deir el-Medina, which in Arabic means the "City Monastery", was given to the site because of the presence there of a Ptolemaic temple dedicated to Hathor and transformed during the Coptic era into a monastery. The village was founded during the Eighteenth Dynasty, in the period of Tuthmosis I, and was called *Set Maat,* which could be translated as "the Place of Truth" or, even better, "the Place of Order". It houses a community of craftsmen and workers who were engaged in the building and decoration of the royal tombs. The studies of the organization of this workers' village, one of the rare urban structures known today in Egypt, and of the tombs in the necropolis, as well as the epigraphic analysis of the elements found in the course of the excavations, among which there are numerous ostraca (pieces of pottery and limestone fragments containing sketches of ornaments or annotations and notes), have made possible a detailed reconstruction not only of the way of life in the settlement, but also of the social and industrial organization of these workers of pharaoh. The village, which occupied an area of about two hectares and, during the Ramessid period, housed a population of about 400 persons, was enclosed in a wall belt of unburned brick and included about 70 dwellings within the walls and about 50 more outside. The houses, of a more or less similar structure, were built of unburned brick and covered with roofs made from planks of palm wood; they consisted of some contiguous small rooms, a terrace which could be reached via an internal

staircase, and sometimes a cellar excavated in the ground. The internal walls were covered with a layer of stucco made of gypsum, limestone and crushed straw which was subsequently whitewashed and painted. A certain space was occupied by a small chapel with a stele intended for the domestic cult of the ancestors and of the goddess Meretseger, "She Who Loves Silence", who personified the Theban Peak and was the protectress of the village. The floors were made of stone, and sometimes they still preserve the marks left by the opening and closing of the wooden entrance doors. Wicker baskets served for the storage of various objects, while foodstuffs and liquids were kept in ceramic vases. The relative abundance of small receptacles for cosmetic products and ointments, as well as of bronze mirrors, shows the importance attributed to the care of the body. The furniture consisted principally of chairs, stools, benches, and small chests. Various remnants of foodstuffs have shown that the principal elements of the workers' diet were cereals and fish, which were

MAIN STREET

N

VILLAGE

NECROPOLIS

ARTIST'S IMPRESSION OF THE SITE OF DEIR EL-MEDINA DURING THE NINETEENTH DYNASTY

VENTILATION AIR INTAKE
VOTIVE NICHE
FALSE DOOR
ROOF STAIRWAY
STORE-ROOM
KITCHEN
STREET
ENTRANCE
CHAPEL
LIVING ROOM
CELLAR

CHAPEL
LIVING ROOM
ROOM
ENTRANCE
STORE-ROOM
KITCHEN

sands and fragments of the mountain covered it until it was recently found. The excavations at the site carried out early in this century by Ernesto Schiaparelli of the Egyptian Museum of Turin brought to light the entire village, perfectly preserved, as well as the adjacent necropolis where, among other finds, the tomb of the architect Kha was found intact and is now reconstructed in the Museum of Turin. At present, excavations and studies of the site are carried out by the Institut Français d'Archeologie Orientale (IFAO), which replaced Schiaparelli's Missione Archeologica Italiana.

distributed to every worker in precise quantities by way of payment for the work done. This diet was supplemented by fruit, vegetables, honey and sometimes meat – generally poultry – which was considered luxury food. The traditional drink was beer made by the fermentation of grains. When the distribution of foodstuff rations, which were the equivalent of wages, was delayed, the workers lodged protests to the superintendent of tombs, who, in his turn, passed them to the vizier, as evidenced by a document written by such a superintendent in the 28th year of the reign of Ramesses III and addressed to the vizier Tô: "... All the foodstuffs to be found in the treasury, the grain deposits, and in the warehouses have been exhausted ... our patron should provide us with means of subsistence since we are dying; actually we are no longer living ..." If such a situation was not corrected within a short time, the workers could organize a strike.

This workers' community of Deir el-Medina existed in isolation, without contact with the outside world, for reasons of discretion and secrecy imposed by the delicate nature of the work of arranging the royal tombs. The community reported directly to the vizier, a functionary who played the role of the pharaoh's prime minister.

In addition, it was controlled by a special corps of guards called *Medjay*, who were stationed outside the village and whose general task

was to guard the necropolis.

The workers, who had the title of "servants of the Seat of Truth", went to work in the Valley of the Kings or the Valley of the Queens using two pathways that are still passable today. Sometimes, when they had to do important and urgent work, they did not return daily to their lodgings but stayed during the whole working week (which in fact lasted ten days) in two small satellite villages situated on the ridge separating the valley of Deir el-Medina from the Valley of the Kings (the so-called hill village) and within the Valley of the Queens. The workers' village of Deir el-Medina was active up to the end of the Twentieth Dynasty, but then it was abandoned, and the desert

Hathor Chapel
Great Pit
Ptolemaic Temple
Temple of Amun
TT no. 3 Pashedu
Site of I.F.A.O. Mission (French Institute of Oriental Archaeology)
Necropolis
Workers Village
TT no. 1 Sennedjem
TT no. 359 Inherkhau
Car Parking

The site of Deir el-Medina

N

0   50   100 metres

131 center right Topographic map of the site of Deir el-Medina, showing the workers' village, the necropolis, a Ptolemaic temple flanked by a chapel dedicated to the goddess Hathor, a small temple dedicated to Amun and a deep cistern of the "Great Well".

131 bottom Also from Sennedjem's tomb, which was a kind of family tomb containing a score of mummies, comes the casket for shawabti of Khons, one of Sennedjem's sons, decorated with pictures of the mummy. The shawabti were statuettes called down by the dead man through the magic formula provided in Chapter 6 of the Book of the Dead, to carry out the most difficult tasks in the Afterlife for him.
(Cairo Museum)

THE TEMPLE OF DEIR EL-MEDINA

132 top *The walls of the temple's inside chapels are decorated with painted bas-reliefs that have preserved some of their original colors.*

Directly to the north of the workers' village there is a small Ptolemaic temple dedicated to Hathor and Maat, to Amenophis, son of Hapu, and to Imhotep; in the Coptic period it was transformed into a monastery, from which the site's present name originated. The temple, built in the third century BC at the time of Ptolemy IV Philopator and Ptolemy VI Philometor (second-third century BC), has been perfectly preserved, including a tall belt of walls made of unburned brick, and the warehouses. Its simple architectural style includes a hypostyle hall with two columns and a vestibule decorated with scenes of Ptolemy VI worshipping various gods; in the left part, one can see the king burning incense in front of the goddess Hathor in the form of a cow. The bas-reliefs of the three chapels

situated behind the vestibule, of which the central one has an entrance decorated with the seven heads of Hathor, and the sanctuary of the goddess, represent, in general, various scenes of sacrifices being offered to gods. In the left chapel there is a representation of a trial by Osiris, a subject which seldom appears in the iconography of buildings dedicated to cults but is represented in tombs or in funerary papyruses. On the opposite wall of the same chapel one can see Ptolemy VIII Euergetes II offering sacrifices to Anubis wearing an unusual mantle. The temple also contained objects pertaining to the cult of the deified rulers Amenophis I, founder of the Eighteenth Dynasty, and his wife Ahmosis Nefertari, who enjoyed particular popularity among the village's inhabitants.

A - Entrance
B - Hypostyle hall
C - Vestibule
D - West chapel
E - Chapel of Hathor
F - East chapel

132 left *The temple of Deir el-Medina is subdivided into three chapels: the central chapel was dedicated to Hathor-Maat, while the eastern chapel (right) was dedicated to Amun-Re-Osiris and the western chapel (left) to Amun-Sokar-Osiris.*

132 center top *The temple of Deir el-Medina was constructed in the third century BC, during the reign of Ptolemy IV, and enlarged under Ptolemy VI and Ptolemy XI in the second and first century BC. Subsequently it was transformed into a Coptic monastery that is the source of the present name of the entire site, which means, in Arabic, "Monastery of the City".*

132 center *A bas-relief representing the goddess Hathor, to whom the temple was dedicated.*

132 bottom *The goddess Hathor, seated on a throne, holds an ankh and a scepter, in the form of a papyrus stem, characteristic of the female deity.*

D

E

F

G

Description of the walls
a - Scenes from the Book of Gates
b - Texts from the Book of the Dead with a scene of senet-*game*
c - Inherkhau and his wife facing kings, queens and princes
d - Scenes from the Afterworld, on three registers (seventeen scenes)
e - The deceased with children in the presence of Ptah and Osiris

f - The deceased in front of mythological creatures, on three registers (fourteen scenes)

E

D

C

B

A

d

b

a

c

BURIAL CHAMBER

F

N

e

G

f

H

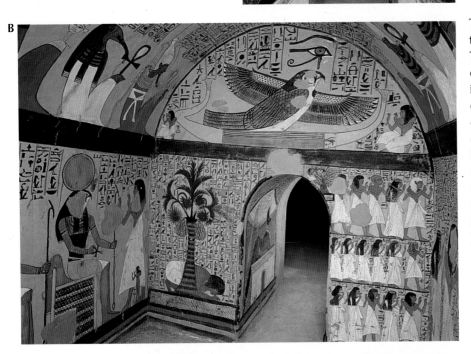

A

PASHEDU
TT no. 3

"Servant in the Place of Truth on the West of Thebes"
Ramesside Period

The tomb of Pashedu, who held the title of "Servant in the Place of the Truth on the West of Thebes", was only recently opened to the public. It is known for the scene shown on the eastern wall next to the entrance door and representing the deceased drinking from a small basin under a large palm-tree. Only the burial chamber is decorated; it is accessible through a small vaulted passage whose walls feature two images of Anubis in the form of a jackal. Other very beautiful scenes are those that adorn the tympanum of the back wall, where one can see Osiris and Horus in the form of falcons in front of a large animated *udjat*-eye supporting candles. In the tympanum of the opposite opening (above the entrance) one can see the god Ptah-Sokaris in the form of a falcon worshipped by Pashedu.

B

A - The narrow passage that leads into Pashedu's burial chamber is decorated with a dual image of Anubis in the form of a jackal crouching on a shrine, with the nekhakha- flail between his hind paws.

B - General view of the wall of the burial chamber: On the tympanum Pashedu and his son Menna respectively worship the god Ptah-Sokaris, in the form of a winged falcon on a boat, surmounted by an udjat-eye, and a group of gods that appears on the north wall. Lower and to the left, Pashedu crouches under a palm-tree, while to the right, arranged on three registers, are portrayed the dead man's attendants. In the left corner of the upper register there is also a representation of the sycamore-goddess. Finally, we

C

can see the initial scene of the lower register of the northern wall, made up of Pashedu, accompanied by a little girl, in the presence of Re-Harakhty and a group of three other gods (Atum, Khepri and Ptah) not visible in the photograph.

C - Pashedu, followed by his wife, Nedjemtebehdet, with two children, and by the attendants arranged on three registers, worships Horus (not visible), while on the walls are transcribed passages from the Book of the Dead. *In the vaulted passage is one of the*

two representations of Anubis in the form of a black jackal.

D - Detail of the dead man's attendants.

D

138

BURIAL CHAMBER

N

PASSAGE

Description of the walls

a - Anubis in the form of a jackal

b - The relatives of Pashedu

c - The dead man and his family worship Horus, in the form of a falcon, and Anubis

d - In the tympanum: the dead man worships Osiris, the udjat-eye, and Horus

e - Pashedu and a girl worship Re-Harakhty, Atum, Khepri and Ptah

f - The dead man quenches his thirst beneath a palm-tree

g - In the tympanum: Ptah-Sokaris on a boat is worshipped by Pashedu.

E

G

H

I

E - Detail of Pashedu's wife, Nedjemtebehdet, portrayed in the typical style of the Ramessid period: the preparation of the wall is rough, but the style, although neglected in the details, is fresh and bright. Nedjemtebehdet wears her hair divided into many small black tresses, and a cloth band on her brow also supports the characteristic cone of scented oils.

F - Detail of the western wall tympanum. A large living udjat-eye supports a torch, while below Pashedu is portrayed in an act of worship.

G - Pashedu with his wife and a daughter on a boat, and before a table of offerings, make a pilgrimage to Abydos.

H - Details of the northern part of the vaulted ceiling with a procession of gods. From the right we see Thoth, followed by Hathor, Re-Harakhty and Neith.

I - Pashedu crouches by a stream in the shade of a palm-tree laden with clusters of dates.

139

THE PRIVATE TOMBS

("TOMBS OF THE NOBLES")

The private tombs of the New Kingdom period in Thebes – usually referred to as "tombs of the nobles" – have been excavated on the sides of the mountain in a rather large area extending between the Valley of the Kings and the Valley of the Queens. They are situated in various necropolises – Dra Abu el-Naga, el-Khokha, Assasif, Deir el-Bahri, Sheikh Abd el-Qurna, Qurnet Murai and Deir

140 top General view of the Theban necropolis. On the right can be seen the necropolises of Assasif, el-Khokha and the hill of Sheikh Abd el-Qurna, which houses the greatest number of tombs.

140 bottom The entrance to the tomb of Ramose (TT no. 55, left) is at the foot of the hill of Sheikh Abd el-Qurna a few hundred meters from the asphalt road leading toward the Valley of the Kings. Further south, on the right, are the entrances to other tombs, including that of Khaemhat (TT no. 57).

el-Medina – and constitute an extraordinary complex of more than 500 tombs decorated with paintings which, unlike those in the royal tombs, also show scenes and moments of daily life, thus enabling us to observe, as in a journey into the past, the daily routine of Egypt 3,500 years ago.

The tombs, whose structure varies according to their date, generally include an outer yard and a funerary chapel intended for the offerings and the private worship of the deceased, preceded by an underground passage or a shaft leading to the burial chamber, usually not decorated. The classical Theban tomb has an inverted T-like plan with a first transversal room, or vestibule, and a second long room with its main axis perpendicular to the previous, or a chapel ending in a niche in which the statue of the deceased was found. Above the entrance there was frequently a pyramidion, of the kind which adorned the Deir el-Medina tombs. On these necropolises numerous

private dwelling-places have been built, in many cases incorporating part of the tombs, which are used as cellars or cowsheds. This phenomenon is not a recent one (it was extensively described by nineteenth-century travelers), but today it is increasingly the cause of very serious problems and of damage to the very delicate wall paintings, both because of the increase in the number of houses and because of the enormous increase in water consumption: in the absence of a drainage and sewerage network, the waste water is absorbed by the limestone which forms the Theban mountain, thus increasing the moisture in the walls of the tombs and producing alterations and flaking of the wall paintings. Presently, only about fifteen tombs are equipped for tourist visits and are open to the public, about ten of them being the most beautiful and best preserved of the entire necropolis. They may be regarded as great masterpieces of the art of the New Kingdom.

KHAEMHAT
TT no. 57

"Royal Scribe, Overseer of the Granaries of Upper and Lower Egypt"
Eighteenth Dynasty

A - Bas-relief representing Khaemhat, "Royal Scribe, Overseer of the Granaries of Upper and Lower Egypt", in an act of worship. The columns of the text transcribe a hymn to Re.

B - Khaemhat, who is represented in high-relief, makes food offerings to the goddess Renenut, the "Lady of the Fertile Land", goddess of the crops and protector of the granaries. The rather refined and elegant style of the decorations of this tomb, which has clear stylistic similarities with that of Ramose (TT no. 55), is typical of the age of Amenophis III.

C - Detail of the masts of two armed transport boats with the shrouds and the halyards to hoist the sails.

D - A chariot drawn by four magnificent horses.

Khaemhat was a dignitary who lived in the reign of Amenophis III and carried the title "Royal Scribe, Overseer of the Granaries of Upper and Lower Egypt". His tomb is situated at the foot of the hill of Sheikh Abd el-Qurna, not far from the Ramesseum and the more famous tomb of Ramose. The tomb is decorated in the "relief" style, in which the paintings are replaced, at least in part, with very fine uncolored sculptures with faintly accented reliefs.

The plan of the tomb is slightly different from usual because the chapel has a vaulted ceiling and continues not with a simple niche but with a proper transverse room with six large statues of the deceased, his bride – Tyti – and relatives. Even the decorative plan includes quite rare scenes and subjects, like the adoration by the deceased of the sun, or the presentation of reports to King Amenophis III, complementing the usual representations of rural labors in the left part of the vestibule, where there are also two statues which represent Khaemhat and his father, Imhotep.

In the chapel, whose decorations are partly destroyed, the themes are essentially mystic and religious, such as the funeral of the deceased and the pilgrimage to Abydos.

There are also inscriptions of a cryptographic nature and passages from the *Book of the Dead* carved at the bottom of the walls next to the opening into the last room.

Description of the walls
a - Agricultural scenes
b - Unloading of a ship; market
c - Niche with statues of the dead man and his family
d - A man leads the herd before the king.
e - Funeral scenes

f - Niches with statues of the dead man and his family
g - Fields of Iaru and pilgrimage to Abydos; sacrificial scenes
h - The dead man and notables of Upper and Lower Egypt rewarded by Amenophis III
i - Agricultural scenes

141

SENNEFER

TT no. 96

"Mayor of the Southern City"
Eighteenth Dynasty - Reign of
Amenophis II

The tomb of Sennefer, "Mayor of the Southern City" – a senior official who lived in the age of Amenophis II – is found on the upper side of the southeastern slope of the Sheikh Abd-el Qurna hill, above that of the vizier Rekhmire (TT no. 100), in a privileged position overlooking the Ramesseum - Ramesses II's great memorial temple - and the alluvial plain of the Nile.

This tomb (the upper chambers of which are inaccessible) is of outstanding beauty. It has a classical "T" plan, but differs from all the other tombs of the Eighteenth Dynasty both in the unusual amplitude of the four-pillar burial chamber and in the fact that all its rooms are decorated, unlike all the other private tombs of the Eighteenth Dynasty (except that of an official who lived in the age of Tuthmosis III, the scribe Amenemhat, owner of tomb no. 82). It was normally the vestibule-chapel complex that was decorated, intended for the cult of the deceased performed by relatives and friends: nobody could penetrate into the burial chamber after the inhumation of the deceased. Only in later periods was the practice of decorating this part of the tomb begun, but always with scenes of a religious kind and related to the underworld.

The real uniqueness of the tomb of Sennefer is not in the fact that the burial chamber is decorated but in its unusual decorative program: the real focus is not so much the underworld as the deceased himself with his wife. The paintings constitute a celebration of the noble couple united by a love that goes beyond

earthly life and is assimilated to the divine one that unites Osiris to Isis, just as Sennefer and his wife are themselves assimilated to the two divinities. Finally, a further stylistic novelty is introduced in the decoration of the burial chamber and of the tomb's antechamber: the ancient artist decided to exploit the natural unevenness of the rock forming the ceiling of the two chambers, in order to confer a three-dimensional effect to the representation of a great pergola from which hang big bunches of grapes. This is an evocation of Osiris's vineyard, linked to the concept of vital strength, of revival and of regenerating power that constitutes one of the most typical prerogatives of the Lord of the Afterlife. The effect produced by the use of this innovative technique was of such beauty that nineteenth-century travelers, deeply impressed, called this hypogeum (considered today one of the highest expressions of the art of ancient Egypt) the "Tomb of the Vineyards".

Sennefer was one of the most influential officials in the court of Amenophis II, who lived in the second half of the fifteenth century BC, an age of great prosperity and wealth for Egypt: after the victorious military campaigns of Tuthmosis III, Amenophis II's predecessor, the country was at the center of a large empire stretching from Asia Minor to the Nile's fourth cataract, in the southern part of present-day Sudan. Sennefer originated from a family of civil servants, court officials and high-ranking priests (his brother Amenemipet, called Pairy, owner of tomb no. 29, was vizier – equivalent to the pharaoh's prime minister): he enjoyed great prestige, beside having considerable personal wealth. Little is known of Sennefer's private life: official documents tell us that he married a woman named Senetnay, of whom, however, there is no mention in the tomb, but who may probably be identified with the lady Merit repeatedly appearing in the paintings. They had two daughters, Mut-Nofret and Tuya, the latter

142-143 View of the burial chamber, with the ceiling, (supported by four pillars), decorated partly with geometric motifs and partly with an extraordinary representation of a vine laden with bunches of grapes to which the artist has given a three-dimensional aspect using the unevenness of the rock surface, earning this tomb the nickname of the "Tomb of the Vineyards". On the pillar in the foreground Sennefer affectionately places his hand on the shoulder of Merit, and on the back wall a priest (not visible) carries out a purification rite before the couple.

143 Sennefer and Merit, seated in the cabin of their boat, make the pilgrimage to Abydos and descend the Nile. In the bow a priest dedicates a table of offerings.

mentioned in the tomb's antechamber together with another woman by the name of Setneferet, about whom we have no precise information.

The prerogatives of Sennefer, "Mayor of the Southern City", capital of the empire and center of religious life, granted him wide powers in the economic management not only of the city but also of the great temples and the huge properties annexed. (The great temple of Amun at Karnak alone had more than 400 gardens and over 200 hectares of tilled soil.)

The numerous titles with which Sennefer is referred to in his tomb not only testify to these manifold temporal powers but also indicate that he must have enjoyed a peculiar and maybe preeminent position among all the court's high officials. It is also possible that Sennefer and his bride were buried not in the tomb on Sheikh Abd el-Qurna hill but in an even more privileged and exclusive spot: in the Valley of the Kings. The discovery in tomb KV no.

42 – intended, possibly, for Tuthmosis II but left unfinished – of numerous pots bearing the name of Sennefer and of his wife might support this hypothesis.

The antechamber

Probably because of its depth and the good quality of the rock in this section of the necropolis, the wall decorations of the burial chamber and of the antechamber of Sennefer's tomb are in a perfect state of preservation, even though the hypogeum has been open to visitors since the beginning of the last century. A steep staircase opening off the yard facing the chapel leads into the antechamber, located 12 meters down, after a sudden elbow bend. It is a small room adjoining the burial chamber, with which it communicates through a narrow opening. The wall paintings of the antechamber show the deceased sitting under a grape-laden pergola, that constitutes the decorative theme of the entire

ceiling, as he attends the presentation of the funerary equipment and of the offerings of linen tissues, torches, a foreleg of beef and bread. The offerings are presented by a procession of priests led by Tuya, one of Sennefer's daughters, who hands her father an amulet with a little heart of lapis lazuli (western wall), while another procession of servants on the eastern wall carry on trays the ornaments of the mummy (collars, two *shawabti*, sandals, a heart-shaped amulet and the funerary mask), the bed and Sennefer's personal belongings, locked up in two small boxes.

On the northern side, beside the door, the deceased and a woman by the name of Setneferet, "much beloved sister and singer of Amun", playing the sistrum, are shown in the act of worshipping Osiris and Anubis, the two major divinities of the Afterlife, no longer visible.

The burial chamber

The splendid burial chamber has a particularly complex decorative program which reflects the life of the deceased and of his wife in the Afterworld. The ceiling, supported by four pillars painted on all sides, takes up the motif of the pergola laden with bunches of grapes, already used in the ceiling of the antechamber, while on the southern side this is replaced by geometrical decorations typical of the ceilings of the Eighteenth Dynasty tombs.

The decorations of the pillars are rather peculiar and always show on three sides Merit handing to Sennefer lotus flowers, perfumed ointments, food, myrrh, protecting amulets, linen bands, necklaces and a sistrum; in one instance only, on the southeastern pillar, we see Merit simply standing in front of the deceased. The scenes figured on the fourth side of each pillar are different: on Pillar One (southwest) we see Sennefer and Merit under a sycamore, on Pillar Two (northwest)

there is a representation of the "goddess of the sycamore" handing water to the couple, overlooked by a double representation of Anubis in canine form, while on Pillars Three (northeast) and Four (southeast) there are two evocations of moments in the rite of the "Opening of the Mouth" (also illustrated in the paintings of the southern side of the eastern wall and on the eastern side of the southern wall), thanks to which the deceased magically recovers the use of his senses and speech. Sennefer is shown on top of an alabaster basin while being cleansed by four priests sprinkling water (Pillar Three) and finally, after his revival, again surrounded by four priests (Pillar Four).

The wall decorations were not painted at random but in a quite precise order, following the ritual orientation of the tomb, according to which the east coincides with the door of the burial chamber. This ritual orientation reflects the journey in the Afterworld of the deceased's

soul, which, after going through different stages, ends with the transformation and regeneration of the deceased and his "appearing in broad daylight".

The scenes start on the western (or more precisely on the northwestern) wall, corresponding to the ritual south, with a representation of Sennefer and Merit making offerings to Osiris-Unnefer, "Lord of the Holy Land, Prince of Eternity", and to Hathor, "Lady of the Western Necropolis". Then follows Sennefer's funeral: the transportation into the necropolis of the deceased's sarcophagus, hauled by four oxen, preceded by servants carrying the funerary equipment locked up in wooden coffers and the offerings, and accompanied by friends and by the highest-ranking officials. Next comes a representation of the details of the funerary rites: the washing and cleansing of the body, the transportation of the canopic jars containing the entrails of the deceased, etc.

On the northern wall – or more precisely on the northeastern, corresponding to the ritual west – we see, in the first portion, a double scene of food offerings to Osiris: Sennefer and Merit are shown facing rich tables of offerings, in front of which the priests carry torches and libations. The scenes are accompanied by texts transcribing the offering formulas. The text accompanying the first scene reads: "Offering the king gives to Osiris, Lord of Eternity, so that he might provide bread and beer, meat and every good and pure thing for the *ka* of Sennefer purified."

The eastern side of the wall shows scenes of river-navigation, preceded by a scene in which Sennefer and Merit worship Anubis and the resurrected Osiris, whose face is painted with the reddish color traditionally used in depicting the living. The nautical scene that comes next (but which from a logical point of view precedes the worshiping) recalls the pilgrimage to Abydos, the "holy" town where, according to tradition, was found the tomb of Osiris, Lord of the Afterlife but at the same time embodiment of the

144 On the four pillars of the burial chamber, the Sennefer-Merit couple is represented no less than fourteen times. It is not known exactly who Merit is: as far as we know from official documents, Sennefer's wife was called Senetnay, but it may be supposed that the two are identical and that Merit –"the Beloved" – is merely the idealization of Senetnay. In the photograph Merit hands to Sennefer, on a tray, a necklace made of gold petals, while with her other hand she supports on her husband's chest a pendant, made up of two hearts, one of gold and the other of silver, on which the cartouches of Amenophis II are etched.

145 top Merit offers Sennefer a goblet containing a beverage. In the upper part of the scene two udjat-eyes are portrayed at the sides of a shenu-sign that has a protective role.

regenerating power and of the concept of resurrection, since he triumphed over death. In the myth of Osiris, the god's body had been dismembered by his evil brother Seth, but was compassionately pieced together by Isis, his wife and a great magician, who succeeded in restoring him to life again and in having with her beloved husband a son: Horus.

The kings of the First Dynasty had themselves buried at Abydos, and those of later dynasties had cenotaphs built for themselves there. In order to take a symbolic part in the resurrection of Osiris, the deceased made a ritual pilgrimage to Abydos in order to assimilate himself with the god. It was Osiris who presided over the divine court of justice and who "weighed" the soul of the deceased, comparing it to the feather of Maat, embodiment of the cosmic order and therefore of divine justice: only after having overcome this trial did the deceased become *makheru*, that is to say "justified", identifying himself with Osiris. So we see Sennefer and Merit aboard their funerary boat painted in green – a color

symbolizing papyrus, but also metaphorically regeneration – sitting under a baldachin together with a priest performing a cleansing rite while they are about to accomplish the ritual pilgrimage. Sennefer's bark is hauled by a second, bigger, craft in which are represented the helmsman, the rowers and the captain who steers downstream to Abydos. The bottom register depicts the journey in the opposite direction and the return to the necropolis. The boat towing Sennefer's boat hoists a rectangular sail to help the rowers sailing upstream all the way to Thebes.

On the southeastern wall, the deceased and Merit are at first shown worshipping Osiris and Anubis, while at the center the scene illustrates Chapter 151 of the *Book of the Dead*: Anubis the divine embalmer, flanked by Isis on his right and Nephthys on his left, attends to Sennefer's mummy, lying on the deathbed, beneath which his *ba*, the soul of the deceased in the shape of a bird, is represented. At the corners of the rectangle in which these scenes are found, we see the

standing figures of Horus's four sons (clockwise: Qebhsenuef, Duamutef, Imset and Hapy), protectors of the canopic jars, and in the lower part are two *shawabti* accompanied by a passage from Chapter 6 of the *Book of the Dead*, including the magic formula by which the deceased was able to call the *shawabti* (a word meaning "the respondent") and order

BURIAL CHAMBER

STAIRWAY

VESTIBULE

RITUAL NORTH

GEOGRAPHICAL NORTH

STAIRWAY

VESTIBULE

145 bottom Section and plan of Sennefer's tomb (TT no. 96). A steep flight of 44 steps leads, with a sharp bend, to the vestibule, located at a depth of twelve meters, which in turn leads into the burial chamber.

PILLARS

3°   4°

BURIAL CHAMBER

2°   1°

PILLARS

A - In the vestibule, a representation of servants bearing the mummy's ornaments on trays: a large menat collar, a second collar and leather sandals, two shawabti, the funeral mask and a heart-shaped amulet painted blue to symbolize lapis lazuli.

B - The architrave of the small opening between the burial chamber and the vestibule is decorated with a double representation of Anubis in the form of a black jackal crouching on a shrine, while the hieroglyphic texts transcribe an invocation to various deities, including Anubis, Mut, Amun-Re and Osiris.

C - Sennefer and Merit are portrayed seated in a conventional attitude. Merit has her hair tied with a band adorned with a large lotus flower, while under the high-backed chairs can be seen two alabaster vessels containing scented oils.

D - Detail of the ceiling of the burial chamber with a geometric decoration of zigzags interspersed with ornate squares.

E - Sennefer, seated under a sycamore with Merit at his feet, inhales the scent of a lotus flower and holds in his hand a sekhem-scepter, symbol of power and authority. In front, on a table, there are three vessels filled with ale around which lotus stems are twined.

F - A different motif of geometric decoration of the ceiling, with simple colored zigzags.

G - The famous "bower decoration" with the bunches of grapes that seem to stand out from the ceiling.

H - Detail of the return journey from Abydos toward Thebes: the boat towing the craft carrying Sennefer and his wife has hoisted its sail to use the wind for its journey up the Nile.

I - Merit offers two white linen bands to Sennefer, who is smelling a lotus flower.

J - A sem-priest, holding in his hand a gold nemset-vessel, purifies Sennefer and his wife.

them to undertake in his stead the heaviest labors in the Afterworld. On the southern end of the wall there is a representation of a peculiar moment of the ceremony of the "Opening of the Mouth": Sennefer and Merit are being cleansed by a *sem*-priest, a very ancient priestly figure of the funerary rite wearing a characteristic leopard skin.

The adjoining scene, with which the southern wall begins (corresponding to the eastern wall of the ritual orientation, at the centre of which is the entrance), shows a priest performing libations and burned offerings in front of the couple. Finally, on the western half of this wall there is a triple representation of Sennefer and Merit – first portrayed in a conventional way sitting on two high-backed chairs, then standing while they get ready to "appear in broad daylight" in order to "see the (solar) disk in its daily journey", and finally symbolically coming out again from the entrance of the burial chamber, whose architrave is overlooked by a double image of Anubis – "the Embalmer" and "Lord of the Holy Land" – in the shape of a black dog smelling a bunch of lotus flowers on top of two chapels, ritual representations of the tomb itself.

NORTH RITUAL

NORTH GEOGRAFICAL

C

D

Description of the walls
***a** - Funeral procession*
***b** - Sennefer and Merit*
***c** - Funeral procession; the deceased before Osiris and Hathor*
***d** - Merit offers Sennefer flowers*
***e** - Sennefer and Merit in the shade of a sycamore tree.*

***f** - Pilgrimage to Abydos*
***g** - The deceased is purified by four priests*
***h** - Merit offers Sennefer two white rolls of linen*
***i** - Sennefer and Merit worship Osiris and Anubis*
***j** - Ritual representation of*

the tomb as indicated in Chapter 151 of the Book of the Dead
***k** - Purification of Sennefer and Merit. The mummy of the deceased and his soul with Anubis, Isis and Nephthys*

REKHMIRE

TT no. 100

"Governor of the Town and Vizier"
Eighteenth Dynasty

148 top Detail of a funeral banquet: a young maidservant helps a lady adorn herself with her jewels.

148 center During the funeral banquet three young musicians play the harp, the lute and the tambourine. The style of this scene, which is extraordinarily elegant, shows traces of archaism typical of the Eighteenth Dynasty.

148 bottom A procession of servants transports the deceased's burial riches.

149 top left Various stages of the work of the goldsmiths (upper register) the tanners and the furriers (lower register).

149 top right A portrait of Rekhmire, "Governor of the Town and Vizier", who lived in the age of Tuthmosis III and Amenophis II.

149 bottom Illustration of the various stages of the preparation and transport of mud bricks, the most widely used construction material, then as now.

The tomb of Rekhmire, located on the upper side of the southeastern slope of the Sheikh Abd el-Qurna hill, a little more than 100 meters beneath the tomb of Sennefer, no. 96, is one of the most outstanding and interesting tombs of the whole Theban necropolis. Rekhmire lived in the time of Tuthmosis III and Amenophis II – an age of great expansion of the empire – and acted as vizier, the highest among the state's offices. Considering his importance, it is not surprising that he had himself built an extraordinary tomb. The inscriptions of the tomb allow us to trace its construction back to the reign of Tuthmosis III but also show that Rekhmire was still living during the reign of Amenophis II.

Even though the tomb of Rekhmire has a rather simple and conventional "T" structure, typical of the Eighteenth Dynasty tombs, it differs from all the others in its imposing dimensions, in the quality of the decoration and in the variety of the iconographic program.

A first transversal hall or vestibule, itself quite large, is followed by a longitudinal hall or chapel stretching out considerably not only in length, along its main south-facing axis, but above all in height: the ceiling starts from three meters, and climbs diagonally until it reaches nine meters. This elevation brings the total decorated surface to 300 square meters.

An architectural peculiarity of this tomb is the absence of a funerary shaft, and this has led to the assumption that Rekhmire was never buried in this tomb but rather in the Valley of the Kings, in some tomb as yet unknown – a privilege granted to the highest-ranking officials who enjoyed the pharaoh's favor.

The paintings are of quite high quality, as is their state of preservation: very good in the first transversal hall, but exceptional in the gigantic chapel. The pictorial style is sometimes the archaic style of the Middle Kingdom tombs, from which it appears to draw inspiration, even though it is more lively and richer in chromatic range, while in other instances the paintings possess a vivacity and a dynamism typical of the second half of the Eighteenth Dynasty. The multiple themes dealt with in the decorative program are also of enormous interest: besides some conventional scenes, many others are absolutely unique, giving us a complete and detailed outline of many aspects of daily life and of the artisan activities of the time. There are also scenes of religious rites, such as the ceremony of the "Opening of the Mouth" or the Beautiful Feast of the Valley, which are the most important among those that took place in the necropolis. Unfortunately, the incredible height of the scenes in the upper registers of the chapel makes their observation almost impossible, and in any case the richness of the iconographic program is such that a thorough analysis would require a special treatment beyond the scope of an introductory guide to the Theban necropolis. For lack of space we shall therefore limit ourselves to the description of the main scenes outlined in the lower and middle registers, which visitors can observe.

The vestibule

On the southwestern wall of the vestibule, which the visitor finds on his left when entering, the products of Upper Egypt are illustrated in five registers while a text describes the goods of the vizier, originally portrayed in the audience hall in the act of inspecting some subordinates (the image is now lost). On the adjoining small western wall there is a long autobiographical text, while on the northwestern wall a scene of great interest shows the tributes from foreign countries, subdivided into five groups and duly registered by the scribes: the inhabitants of the mysterious land of Punt with incense trees, baboons, monkeys and animal hides; the inhabitants of Kefti, a territory probably to be identified with

today's island of Crete, carrying pots and cups; the Kushites or Nubians, represented with animals typical of equatorial Africa's fauna (giraffes, leopards, baboons, monkeys and dogs), offering ivory, animal hides and gold; the Retenus or Syrians, bringing pots, carts, and weapons, besides various animals (horses, a bear and an elephant); and a fifth group uniting diverse foreign populations from different countries, among whom can be seen women with negroid features leading their children by the hand. On the eastern side of the southern wall, Rekhmire (the image of the vizier is now lost) inspects the tributes from Lower Egypt and the workshops of the craftsmen working in the temples, while on the eastern wall several of

his relatives are shown. On the eastern side of the northern wall the products coming from the Mediterranean strip of Lower Egypt are shown with scenes of wine-making, fishing and hunting.

The chapel

The paintings of the chapel are undoubtedly the most interesting and the best preserved of the whole tomb. On the western wall the deceased is first shown supervising the gathering and the preparation of the food provisions allotted to the temple and their distribution, in a series of scenes arranged in six registers, while in the

A - The chapel of Rekhmire's tomb is made up of a narrow corridor with walls rising to a height of nine meters; the surface – about 300 square meters – is completely decorated.

B - Bearers of tributes from foreign countries offer elephant tusks, valuable skins, ostrich eggs and feathers, a baboon and a monkey.

C - A splendid giraffe, portrayed with a monkey climbing its neck, was part of the tributes.

D - A stage of the weighing and recording of the gold and silver under the control of a scribe who records the amount weighed.

E - The different stages of working and decorating metal vessels.

F

G

h

i

j

k

H

I

following series of scenes, arranged in eight registers, are represented all the labors carried out by the craftsmen who worked for Amun's temple: potters, carpenters, decorators, goldsmiths, sculptors and masons busy manufacturing bricks of unburned clay (making use of processes employed up to the present) and transporting them for the building of a great inclined plane, while some sculptors are busy constructing two colossal statues of red granite. The following scenes, arranged in ten registers, are of a funerary character and illustrate the funeral procession heading for the necropolis, the setting up of obelisks, the catafalque hauled by nine friends of the deceased, the pilgrimage to Abydos, the cleansing of the deceased, and scenes of dance and of ritual slaughter of beasts.

On the narrow background wall we can see a niche in which a stele was found (now in the Louvre Museum)

F - In a pond surrounded by trees, the workers draw the water used to make the earth into a paste and, with a mould (seen on the right), to make the unburned bricks.

G - The wall at the back of the chapel ends with a false door over which is a niche in which a stele was originally placed.

H - The vizier Rekhmire, with the **sekhem**-*scepter in his hand, and his wife, Merit.*

I - A young musician plays the tambourine.

J - During the funeral banquet a maidservant serves a goblet of drink to a lady.

K - A large cargo boat, with unfurled sails and the oarsmen at work, goes up the Nile.

Description of the walls
a - The deceased superintends the collecting of Upper Egypt's taxes; weighing of the gold.
b - Inscription
c - Tributes of the foreign populations
d - Preparation and storing of food
e - Artisans, smiths and bricklayers at work
f - The deceased superintending the activities of craftsmen and workers
g - Funeral procession
h - Hathor-Imentit, Anubis and Osiris
i - The deceased and his wife before the table of offerings
j - False door, inscriptions and niche
k - Scenes of offering and purification
m- Scenes of life and of cultivation in a garden
m- Funeral banquet; scenes of musicians
n - The deceased returns from a royal audience; ships
o - Hunting scenes in the desert
p - Grape harvest; preparation and storing of food
q - Scenes of country life (damaged); the deceased superintends collection of Lower Egypt's taxes

and, below, a false door – a decorative element dating back to the Old Kingdom, symbolically leading into the Afterworld. Paintings, accompanied by columns of texts transcribing the formulas of the offerings, represent the deceased bowing down before Osiris while Rekhmire's son Menkeperreseneb gives offerings to the deceased father and to his wife Merit. Finally, on the eastern wall of the chapel we find Menkeperreseneb and two other sons of Rekhmire – Amenophis and Senusert – in the presence of their deceased father and mother. In the following scenes are shown, in ten registers, the rites carried out in front of the statue of the deceased, with scenes of ritual slaughter of beasts, of cleansing, and of preparation of the food in front of the deceased sitting on a high-backed chair, with the representation of a magnificent garden, a pool and a boat. Then comes a beautiful scene, arranged in ten registers, of the funerary banquet, during which the deceased's sons and daughters hand flower wreaths to Rekhmire and to his wife while musicians, both males and females, wearing bright clothes, play diverse instruments among which we see lutes, tambourines, flutes, harps and castanets, while the guests eat sitting on mats and are waited on by numerous servants. Finally, in the last series of scenes, which completes the decorative program of the eastern wall of the chapel, we witness a boat journey undertaken by the deceased in order to receive a high decoration from Pharaoh Amenophis II, a further scene of offering of flowers to Rekhmire by his son, and an audience granted by the vizier to dignitaries and petitioners.

Though brief and necessarily incomplete, this description of the paintings in the tomb of Rekhmire nevertheless gives an idea of the complexity and the completeness of the decorative program of this superb work of art from the first half of the Eighteenth Dynasty, in which archaic and manneristic tendencies are often softened and transcended by the extraordinary talent of the artists who worked there.

NAKHT

TT no. 52

"Scribe, Astronomer of Amun"
Eighteenth Dynasty

A

B

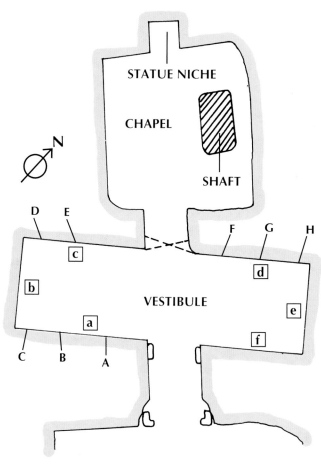

Description of the walls
a - *Scenes of country life*
b - *False door; the goddess Nut gathers the offerings*

c - *Funeral banquet*
d - *Hunting and fishing scenes; grape harvest and preparation of the wine*
e - *Bearers of offerings*

and priests before Nakht and his wife
f - *Purification of the offerings before the deceased*

The tomb of Nakht was the subject of an experimental restoration carried out at the end of the 1980s with the purpose of finding a technique to provide adequate protection to the tombs' paintings while also improving the condition of the tombs themselves. Unfortunately, the relatively sophisticated technology used in the tomb of Nakht – requiring complete insulation with sheets of glass of all the vestibule walls, the only painted part of the tomb – turned out to be too expensive and difficult for use on a large scale.

Represented on the walls, besides scenes of offerings and funeral rites, are moments from rural life having to do with the cultivation of grain, digging of small canals for irrigation, harvest, fishing and hunting in the Nile Delta. On the left wall there is a stele on which are depicted servants

A - Sowing: a peasant strews seeds on the ground from a container. They are planted in the ground by a second farmer who assists with an appropriate wooden instrument.

B - Two farmers plow the fields with a wooden plow pulled by two oxen.

C - Two groups of peasants, using wooden implements, throw the threshed grain into the air to winnow it.

D - A maidservant helps three ladies to adorn themselves with jewels.

C

D

E - By its charm and elegance, this has become one of the most famous scenes of all ancient Egyptian paintings: three young musicians accompany the funeral banquet, playing the harp, the lute and a wind instrument. The musician in the center, who plays a kind of lute, is portrayed, for the first time in Egyptian painting, almost completely naked.

G

F - Splendid and fine detail of Nakht's wife holding a small bird.

G - A double scene of hunting birds in the marshes. Nakht is portrayed, with his wife and two small sons in a papyrus boat, grasping the hunting stick.

H - This group of scenes relates to the preparation of food and drink. In the upper register two peasants are gathering grapes, while others press them; the must produced in this way is then stored in conical jars. In the lower register servants

drag a net that contains a great number of birds, the result of a day's hunt in the marshes. The birds are carefully plucked, cleaned and prepared for cooking.

and two women presenting offerings. The theme of the offerings is repeated in the paintings lining the entrance, showing offerings of food to the deceased and his bride, Tawi, who carried the title "Singer of Amun", while in the next scene the couple make offerings to Amun. On the lower part of the wall, on the left side, is portrayed the funeral banquet with the famous image of three singers, which for the first time in Theban painting features female nudity.

H

MENNA
TT no. 69

*"Scribe of the Fields of the Lord
of the Two Lands of Upper and
Lower Egypt"*
Eighteenth Dynasty

In the tomb of Menna – similar in form, style and dimensions to that of Nakht (TT no. 52) – all the classic themes of Theban painting of the period are represented, but the more notable paintings principally illustrate agricultural labors, spread across five levels which cover the entire left lateral wall of the vestibule (the same

Description of the walls
a - Agricultural scenes
b - The deceased and his wife in the presence of Osiris
c - The deceased and his wife, funeral banquet (fragmentary)
d - Bearers of offerings and funeral procession
e - The deceased before the judgment of Osiris
f - Niche with statues of the deceased and his wife

g - Menna with his family hunting and fishing in the marshes
h - Pilgrimage to Abydos
i- The deceased and his wife receive offerings and a list of the ritual offerings
j - Stelae in three registers: a) the deity of the West; b) seated couples; c) the deceased and his wife in an act of worship
k - Offering scenes

A

B

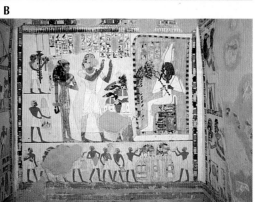

A - The tomb of Menna who bore the title of Scribe of the Fields of the Lords of the Two Lands of Upper and Lower Egypt contains many scenes relating to agricultural labours. On this wall, arranged on four registers, we see different stages of reaping and of the wheat harvest, an operation carried out under the supervision of the scribes who scrupulously record the amount.

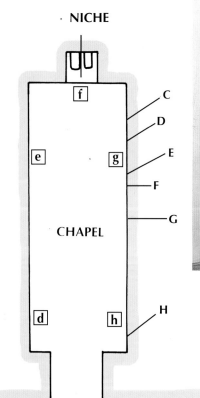

NICHE

f

C

D

e   g   E

F

G

CHAPEL

d   h   H

c   i

VESTIBULE

b   j   I

a   k

N

D

B - The deceased and his wife, before a table of offerings, worship the god Osiris seated on a throne inside a chapel.

C, D - A young daughter of Menna picks the scented lotus flowers (C), while another carries lotus flowers and the birds that have been caught (D).

E - *Magnificent naturalistic detail of life in the marshes among the papyrus and lotus plants, which swarm with life and where many types of birds lay their eggs. At right can be seen a rodent and a cat dangerously close to a nest and, up above, two butterflies.*

F, G - *A dual fishing and hunting scene in the marshes, similar to that portrayed in Nakht's tomb (TT no. 52). Menna stands on a papyrus boat, accompanied by his* wife and sons. On the right he fishes with a harpoon and is portrayed catching two fish (detail in F); on the left he brandishes a stick for hunting and catching birds, while the birds take off from a thicket of papyrus. Given the extraordinary stylistic similarities, it is probable that the tombs of Menna and Nakht were the work of the same artist, who probably worked at the beginning of the reign of Amenophis III.*

G

E

H

F

H - *In the upper register there is a representation of the pilgrimage to Abydos with the fleet of boats returning to Thebes. The lower registers are dedicated to the rites carried out before the mummy, and in particular to the ceremony of the "Opening of the Mouth".*

position as that of the same subject in the tomb of Nakht). The harvest and gathering of grain, closely supervised by the scribe, are shown along with more intimate scenes like a little girl taking a thorn out of a friend's foot, or a mother cradling a newborn child under a tree, which seem to be real renderings of everyday life. On the lower part of the wall of the vestibule (left side) the deceased, followed by his bride, Henut-taui, is represented in the presence of Osiris, seated inside his shrine. On the right wall of the chapel a splendid scene depicts the deceased hunting birds and fishing in the marshes on boats of papyrus, accompanied by his bride, while on the opposite wall there is a complete representation of the funeral of the deceased.

I

I - *On the western wall of the vestibule is a stele subdivided into three registers. Re-Harakhty is depicted in the upper register with the main gods of* the funeral cult, while the middle register has a double representation of the deceased with his wife, Henut-taui.*

RAMOSE
TT no. 55

"Governor of the Town and Vizier"
Eighteenth Dynasty

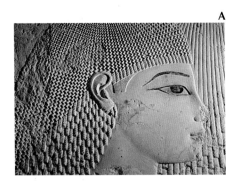

A

The tomb of Ramose, a very high dignitary during the reigns of Amenophis III and Amenophis IV, is placed chronologically after that of Khaemhat (TT no. 57) and, as in the latter's tomb, the decorations here are "in relief".

The tomb is situated at the foot of the hill of Sheikh Abd el-Qurna, not far from the tomb of Khaemhat, and is unfinished because its proprietor probably had to follow the pharaoh in the Amarnan adventure and have another tomb constructed at Akhetaten, the new capital founded by Amenophis IV/Akhenaten.

The architecture of the tomb, which has a traditional "T" plan, seems influenced by a form of gigantism, the dimensions of both the vestibule and the chapel greatly exceeding the customary ones. Some of the representations in relief are extremely refined and the details are particularly elaborate, but the style is clearly of a later date than that of the tomb of Khaemhat and introduces some motifs which were to be developed in the art of the succeeding Amarna period.

The decorations in relief of the two walls which line the entrance to the vestibule, whose ceiling is supported by 32 columns, have as their theme the funeral banquet, while the left wall is decorated with celebrated colored paintings of the deceased's funeral, with crying women, the funeral court, and the funeral furniture which was supposed to be

A - Portrait of a guest at Ramose's banquet. The large scenes of the funeral banquet are sculpted simply in relief on limestone slabs without use of colors except to show the eyes of the figures. Despite their rigid, conservative style, these scenes are distinguished by an elegance and an unequaled stylistic purity, and constitute one of the highest manifestations of ancient art.

B - Detail of a large scene of Ramose's obsequies; this is the only painted scene in

B

C

D

all the tomb: the servants carry the burial riches of the deceased, which will subsequently be placed in the burial chamber.

C - A group of women with their hair loose, as a sign of mourning, lament the death of Ramose, lifting their arms at the passing of the sarcophagus, depicted in the upper register. This scene, considered a masterpiece of Eighteenth Dynasty art, is marked by a lively style

that gives expression to the feeling of grief in face of death.

D - Detail of the scene of purification of Ramose, "Governor of the Town and Vizier", who lived in the age of Amenophis III and Amenophis IV.

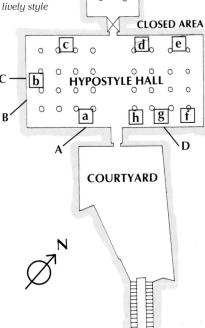

CHAPEL

INTERNAL HALL

CLOSED AREA

HYPOSTYLE HALL

c b d e a h g f

C

B

A

D

COURTYARD

N

Description of the walls
a - Funeral banquet
b - Funeral procession
c - The deceased makes an offering to Amenophis IV and to the goddess Maat
d - The deceased before Amenophis IV and queen Nefertiti followed by dignitaries
e - Ramose is hailed and receives foreign delegations and

garlands of flowers from the temple
f - Priests before the deceased and his family and ritual list of offerings
g - Three maidens with sistra before the deceased and his wife. Purification of the statue of Ramose
h - The deceased, with his wife and bearers of offerings, burn incense

deposited in the tomb. The lower wall of the vestibule, off which opens the entrance to the chapel (inaccessible), has two representations of Ramose in the company of Amenophis IV: the scene on the left in which Ramose offers flowers to the king and to the goddess Maat is in the classic style, while in the scene on the right we can

clearly distinguish the typical Amarna style. Here the king and the queen take part in the ceremonies in honor of the deceased.

KHONSU
TT no. 31

"First Prophet of Menkheperre"
Eighteenth Dynasty

This tomb, TT no. 31, was built for Khonsu, called To, "First Prophet of Menkheperre Tuthmosis III", and is decorated with beautiful scenes of the feast of the god Montu. On one side the deceased (depicted as a priest) and his brother spread incense and make offerings to the boat of Montu; on the opposite side, in a kiosk, the deceased makes offerings to the boat of Tuthmosis III, which arrives at Armant (a site located to the south of Thebes and the birthplace of the god Montu) and is then brought by the priests to the temple. Another wall shows scenes representing the deceased, his wife and Usermontu, the vizier, brought by Harsiesis for trial by Osiris, Isis and Nephthys, with the ritual weighing of the soul in the presence of Maat, goddess of justice and cosmic order, and the various divinities. At the bottom appears a funeral procession with crying people near the pyramidal tomb, a detail extremely important in giving us an idea of the original look of the chapel-tombs of Deir el-Medina. The northern wall of the tomb displays the feast of Tuthmosis III; the procession of the royal boat in front of the temple, received by the priests and priestesses; and herdsmen and shepherds with dogs offering cows and goats with the property symbol of Tuthmosis III to the deceased and his wife and family. There is also a scene of two people on their knees, praying under the trees. The ceiling of the passage to the inner chamber is decorated with grapes, while that of the inner chamber itself has a naturalistic decoration of ducks with their wings spread and three locusts. The niche is decorated with interesting scenes, of which one depicts the deceased offering a bouquet of flowers to Nebhepetre Mentuhotep (Eleventh Dynasty), who wears the white crown of Upper Egypt and grips a scepter, symbol of power.

A

B

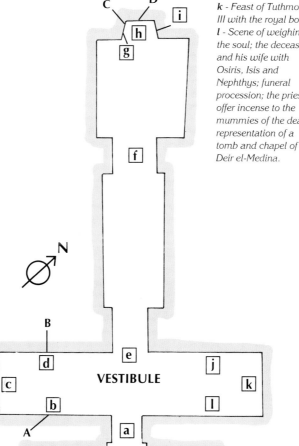

Description of the walls

a - The deceased, his wife and children worship Re. Ceiling decorated with birds.
b - Representation of Montu's bark; priests in a sacrifice to Montu's bark; Montu's bark in the kiosk.
c - Continuation of the procession of Montu's bark.
d - Priests carry Montu's barque; pillar of the temple of Montu (partial).
e - Architrave: offerings of incense to Osiris, Hathor and Re-Harakhty.
f - Ceiling decorated with birds and three locusts.
g - Khonsu, in priestly dress, offers lotus and papyrus to the pharaoh with the white crown (Upper Egypt).
h - The deceased, in priestly dress, makes offerings to Osiris and Anubis.
i - Khonsu, in priestly dress, makes offerings to the goddess Hathor-Imentit.
j - The deceased and his family before Osiris and Anubis.
k - Feast of Tuthmosis III with the royal boat.
l - Scene of weighing of the soul; the deceased and his wife with Osiris, Isis and Nephthys; funeral procession; the priests offer incense to the mummies of the dead; representation of a tomb and chapel of Deir el-Medina.

A - A boat propelled by five oarsmen sails on the lake of the temple of Montu, a war deity originating in ancient Per-Mont (the present-day Armant), a few kilometers south of Luxor.

B - A group of priests carry a simulacrum of the boat of Montu on their shoulders into the temple.

C - The deceased (not visible) offers flowers to the king Nebhepetre Mentuhotep.

D - The deceased carries out a fumigation before Osiris and Anubis.

C

D

USERHAT
TT no. 51

"First Prophet of the Royal Ka of Tuthmosis I"
Nineteenth Dynasty

A

SHAFT

CLOSED

| c | | d | e |
| b | VESTIBULE | g | f |

C

D

| a | COURTYARD |

Description of the walls
a - Stelae with fragments of the funeral ceremony prior to the mummification; lower down, text of the offering
b - Weighing of the soul; representation of Osiris and Hathor; the deceased worships falcon-headed Re-Harakhty; funeral ceremony before the mummy
c - Men bearing gifts; the deceased, leaving the temple, worships the royal boat; priests with flabellum and the cartouche of Tuthmosis I
d - The deceased with two women and a son makes an offering to Osiris and to two gods

e - Priests with grieving women drink and make an offering to the deceased and his wife
f - The deceased with two women receives figs and fruit from the goddess of the sycamore; over the two women, the representation of the two ba; representation of birds; pilgrimage to Abydos; the deceased and his wife before Osiris and Anubis
g - Scene of worship; in the kiosk, Anubis, Osiris and Thoth; purification of eight priests for work; the deceased before the offerings

Tomb no. 51 was constructed for Userhat, called Neferhabef, "First Prophet of the Royal *Ka* of Tuthmosis I" (not to be confused with the homonymous proprietor of tomb no. 56, who carried the title of "Royal Scribe"), in the period of Sethos I. This is one of the most beautiful Theban tombs and is characterized by a series of representations of the owner, his bride and his mother in vivid colors. The eastern wall is decorated with very graceful scenes: the deceased, his wife Hatshepsut (also called Shepset) and his mother are seated under a fig tree with three small birds perching on its branches, while overhead fly three spirits in the form of birds with human heads. The tree-goddess pours water for drinking, and serves bread, apples and figs for eating. A double subscene represents the ritual pilgrimage to Abydos and the deceased and his wife in front of Anubis and Osiris, principal deities of the Underworld. On the southern wall are scenes of adoration and purification while the god Thoth, the divine scribe, presents to Osiris and Anubis his report on the life of the deceased, who in turn is represented in an act of worship to Montu and the goddess Meretseger. The southern wall on the left displays Userhat brought to justice by Anubis, the scene of weighing of the soul with the deceased on his knees before Osiris and the western divinities, and the

A - Candles for the Beautiful Feast of the Valley and offerings are presented to Userhat and his wife, Hatshepsut.

B - Two sem-priests, dressed in the distinctive leopard skins, carry out a purification rite and fumigations before the deceased, while a group of women lament his death.

C - On the eastern wall of the vestibule, the deceased is depicted with his wife, Hatshepsut,

called Shepset, and his mother, Tausert, before the goddess of the Sycamore, a tree that was considered to be one of the manifestations of Hathor and of Nut.

D - Userhat, "First Prophet of the Royal Ka of Tuthmosis I", in an act of worship before the table of the offerings.

funeral procession. On the northern wall a group of crying women draws the attention of the visitor while the deceased, with two women and a son, pours out a salve as a gift to Osiris, accompanied by two goddesses, and on a brazier presents an offering to Tuthmosis I and Ahmosis Nefertari. The northern wall on the right displays the procession for the feast of Tuthmosis I and Userhat, who on leaving the temple, worships the boat and the royal statue in black representing Osiris, accompanied by fan-carriers and crying women. The second room, with four pillars and no decorations, leads to the funeral shaft.

B

C

D

BENIA
TT no. 343

*"Overseer of Works,
Child of the Nursery"*
Eighteenth Dynasty

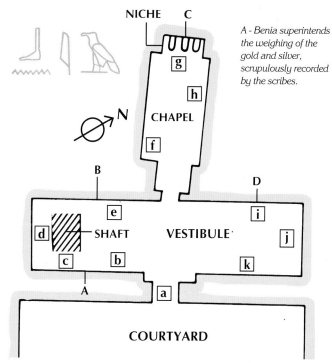

NICHE   C

g

h

CHAPEL

f

N

B

D

e

i

d   **SHAFT**   **VESTIBULE**

j

c

b

k

A

a

COURTYARD

A - Benia superintends the weighing of the gold and silver, scrupulously recorded by the scribes.

B - The musicians enliven the funeral banquet, playing before the deceased's parents, seated in front of the table of offerings, and their guests.

C - Three painted limestone statues, arranged in the niche of the chapel, represent the deceased (in the center) with his mother, Tirurak, and his father, Irtonena.

D - Benia, "Overseer of Works", seated before a table of offerings, inspects the bearers of offerings (cattle, birds, fish, lotus flowers and a variety of food), distributed over three registers.

This tomb, TT no. 343, belonged to Benia, called Pahekmen, an official who lived during the Eighteenth Dynasty and carried the title of "Overseer of Workers, Child of the Nursery".

In the first room a number of scenes are shown: the deceased, with various types of food in front of him, offers two roast ducks on a brazier;

A

B

C

the deceased sits on a chair in front of nine people, arranged in three rows, who bring offerings; a rich table of offerings. On the other wall the deceased, seated, wields a stick and inspects three rows of bringers of offerings: livestock, fish, birds, lotus flowers, food and vegetables.
Entering from the left, the owner of the tomb is shown checking three ledgers regarding the number of ebony, ivory, silver and gold rings and the treasure, all of which are then weighed on a scale, with a counterweight shaped as a small calf, while two scribes write down the weights.
On the opposite wall there is a graceful scene with the deceased seated in front of a rich table bearing offerings presented by a priest.
In the second part of the same scene a banquet is shown, with musicians – a harpist and a lute player – followed by three applauding men. The mother and the father of the deceased tower over this scene. The mother affectionately embraces her husband; under her seat is a mirror.

D

The western wall is composed of a false door, painted in red to simulate granite.
The eastern wall has a stele on the edges of which the deceased is shown on his knees, giving offerings and performing a ritual ceremony. The hallway is decorated with the funeral procession in the presence of the goddess of the West, with the pilgrimage to Abydos, and with scenes of offerings and the "Opening of the Mouth" ceremony, by which life was traditionally restored to the deceased.
The niche contains the statues of the deceased, placed between his mother, Tirukak, on his right, and his father, Irtonena, on his left.

Description of the walls
a - Fragments of conferring of a title; the deceased at worship
b - The deceased worshipping before offerings
c - Weighing and storing of the gold and the turquoises
d - Stelae with texts; alongside, the deceased kneeling in an act of offering
e - The deceased's parents before the table of offerings, with musicians and male guests; the deceased before the table of offerings, with a man making an offering to him
f - Funeral procession and offerings to the goddess Hathor Imentit with was-scepter; the deceased before the table of offerings
g - Niche with statues of the deceased, his mother and father
h - The deceased before the table of offerings; offerings, purification; ceremony of the "Opening of the Mouth"
i - The deceased, seated, inspects the herds and various country products
j - Stele, surmounted by two udjat-eyes; alongside, the deceased kneeling in an act of offering
k - The deceased, before the table of the offerings, receives gifts

ROUTES AND TRAILS OF THE THEBAN MOUNTAIN

ITINERARY NO. 1
From Deir el-Medina to the Valley of the Queens
Duration: approximately one hour

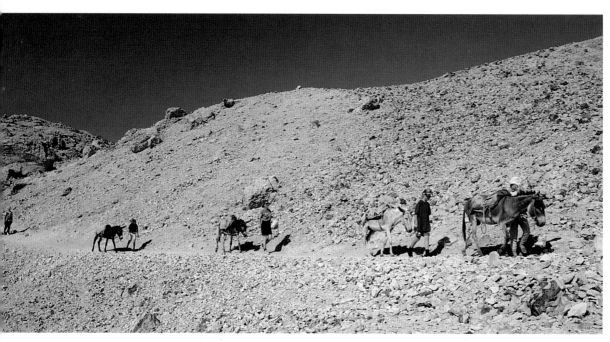

160 *A group of tourists follow the age-old path which leads from Deir el-Medina to the Valley of the Queens and the temple of Deir el-Bahri. Donkeys are still a great help, as they were to nineteenth-century travellers too.*

The route: Leaving the craftsmen's village of Deir el-Medina on the left, you take a very well-defined uphill path which runs to the west. After a few minutes' walk you arrive at the summit of a small hill. At this point the path forks in two directions: the right path runs north and rises at a considerable slope (see itinerary no. 2); the left path gently descends to follow the bottom of a small valley, known as Valley of the Dolmen, because in a hollow which opens on its northern side there is a pile of rocks which resembles a dolmen. Continuing down into the Valley of the Dolmen, after a few minutes you will see on the left two stelae carved in the stone and a votive niche from the period of Ramesses III, followed by an ample shelter used by hermits during the Coptic period – originally a rocky sanctuary dedicated to the god Ptah and the cobra-goddess Meretseger, personification of the Theban Peak: a place of worship and prayer which the workers of the pharaoh erected along their path. Continuing, the Valley of the Dolmen opens up and joins the main wadi of the Valley of the Queens, where you arrive a little farther on and continue on the main path.

If, instead, you take a secondary path which starts from the northern side of the Valley of the Dolmen, a few hundred meters before the opening to the Valley of the Queens, you arrive after a few minutes at the ruins of an ancient Coptic monastery called Deir Rumi, having crossed a clay bank in which can be found numerous marine fossils, evidence of the presence of a prehistoric ocean. The monastery, on a small rocky spur, was built around the fourth century AD by the hermits who inhabited the area.

After the visit to the monastery, follow a path which again leads to the bottom of the main wadi of the Valley of the Queens. From this point it is possible to visit the Valley of the Queens and then return by taxi to the point of departure.

161 top The mountain of Thebes is made of limestone dating back to the Tertiary Era. It is not uncommon to find marine fossils in the rock, like this lamellibranch, attesting to the time when the region was covered by the sea, some 40 million years ago.

161 bottom This curious rock formation is known as "the dolmen".

MAP OF THE PATHS OF THE THEBAN MOUNTAINS

A Ancient path of the workers from the village to the Valley of the Queens
B Ancient path of the workers from the village to the Valley of the Kings
C Path to the Theban Peak
D Path of the Western Valley
E Path of Deir el-Bahri
F Connection from Deir el-Bahri to the Valley of the Kings

ITINERARY NO. 2
From Deir el-Medina to the Theban Peak and the Valley of the Kings
Duration: approximately three hours

The route:
Starting from the summit of the small hill above Deir el-Medina (see itinerary no. 1), follow a path which climbs steeply northward. After about ten minutes you pass a fork from which a small path leads to a rocky spur with a splendid view of the whole area of Deir el-Medina.

A few hundred meters on you arrive at level ground, from which can be seen the surrounding countryside all the way to the Valley of the Queens. If you look carefully, you can see crumbling stone walls; this is the hill station with the remains of the barracks of an ancient guard post which controled access to the royal necropolises. After about 500 meters, at the bottom of a rocky outcrop, another level path starts on the right to the complex of temples at Deir el-Bahri. However, in order to continue our itinerary, we must follow the uphill path to the crest of the mountain chain. Here, in a space which dominates the Nile plain and the Valley of the Kings, can be seen the remains of many houses. This is the hill village, a sort of satellite of the main village of Deir el-Medina which, at times when the weather was extremely hot, or when the work was particularly arduous, permitted the workers involved in the construction of the tombs in the Valley of the Kings to make use of houses closer and more rapidly accessible than those in Deir el-Medina.

Three paths leave the hill village: the first descends toward the Valley of the Kings; the second leads to the western branch of the Valley of the Kings, also known as the Western Valley; and the third climbs to the summit of the Theban Peak. The ascent from this crossing to the Peak takes around half an hour.

At the point of departure, on the right, there is a small rocky sanctuary

162 top A view of the ruins of the Coptic monastery of Deir Rumi, built at the entrance to the Valley of the Queens around the fourth century AD.

162 bottom In ancient times laborers made their way every day along the path linking Deir el-Medina with the Valley of the Kings. Along the path stands

a small sanctuary dedicated to Ptah and to the goddess Mertseger, to whom the labourers were particularly devoted dedicated by the workers to the god Ptah, while on the surrounding stone walls can be observed various graffiti, one of which mentions "the water fallen from the sky" – perhaps a rain of exceptional importance. The path climbs and at a few points becomes very steep, but after a couple of tight spots you arrive without further

163 top At a certain point along the path from Deir el-Medina to Deir el-Bahri and the Valley of the Kings, travelers walk along the edge of a spectacular cliff, over 100 meters high.

163 center From the top of the cliff there is a wonderful view of the Deir el-Bahri site below: to the right is the temple of Nebhepetre Mentuhotep, in the center the temple of Thutmosis III and to the left the great temple of Hatshepsut, flanked by the shrine of Hathor.

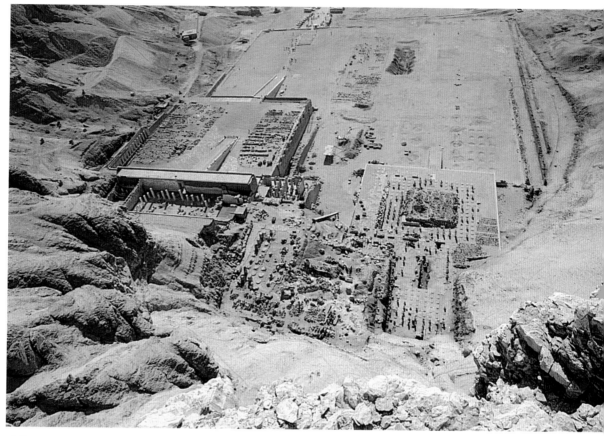

difficulties at the Theban Peak, crossing a clay bank very rich in fossils since in ancient times it was part of a coral reef. The countryside is magnificent, and the view embraces the Valley of the Kings, which extends further down, as well as all the Theban necropolises. On the way back, walk down the same path to the hill village. From there, continue along the path which descends, leading north, and, after passing the tomb of Tuthmosis III, cut in a narrow crack in the rock to the left of the path, you arrive at the heart of the Valley of the Kings, at the tomb of Sethos I and the area occupied until 1991 by the rest-house, now moved outside the archaeological site.

163 bottom This photo shows the path which climbs to the top of the pyramid-shaped mountain of Thebes, overlooking the Valley of the Kings. In the foreground is the hill village perched on the ridge which separates Deir el-Medina from the Valley of the Kings. The laborers who worked in the royal tombs often lived here during the working week, rather than walk longer distances every day.

AMUN
Divinity, "king of the gods", depicted as a human being with two tall plumes overhanging his headdress, or sometimes as a ram, his sacred animal. Together with the goddess Mut and the god Khonsu, he formed the "Theban Triad". He had also been assimilated to the god Re and worshiped as Amun-Re. Thebes was the main seat of his worship.

ANKH
Handled cross, symbol of life and of vital strength.

ANUBIS
Jackal-headed deity, presides over the embalming and accompanies the dead to the Afterlife.

ATUM
Divinity representing the sun as Atum-Re (the demiurge of Heliopolitan cosmology) and above all indicating the star at its setting.

BA
One of man's souls, depicted as a bird with human head.

BOOK OF THE DEAD
A series of 190 "chapters" with magic-ritual wordings, illustrated with sketches, intended to assure the deceased of his survival in the Underworld. The wording was inscribed on papyruses and placed beside the deceased: in the Late Period, spells and drawings were traced on the linen bandages wrapping the mummies.

BOOK OF GATES
A collection of magical/religious texts thanks to which the dead could pass through the portals of the kingdom of Osiris.

CANOPIC JARS
Four vessels holding the lungs, the stomach, the intestines and the liver removed from the body of the deceased. The entrails were placed under the protection of Horus's four sons (Imsety, Hapy, Duamutef, Qebhsenuef), and the jars were sealed by covers in the shape of these divinities.

CARTOUCHE
An ellipsoidal line, originally representing a rope ring with a knot at the base, inside which the name of the pharaoh is written. The use of the cartouche, symbolizing the universal power of the sun-god, and hence of the pharaoh, is reserved to the two most important names out of the five the pharaoh possessed: the nomen (preceded by the title "Son of Re") and the praenomen given at the time of coronation (preceded by the title "King of Upper and Lower Egypt").

DJED
Pillar, symbol of stability and duration. This very ancient amulet related to Osiris, was also used for the protection of the mummies, to whose neck it was suspended.

ENNEAD
The nine deities of the cosmogony of Heliopolis: Atum, Shu, Tefnet, Geb, Nut, Osiris, Isis, Seth and Nephthys.

FIELDS OF IARU
Fields of Osiris's kingdom, a trans-position into the Underworld of the green agricultural areas of the Nile Delta, where the souls of the deceased worked.

GEB
Personification of the earth and husband of Nut.

GESTATION
Period preceding the rebirth of the soul.

HELIOPOLIS
City in Lower Egypt, whose ancient Egyptian name was On (the pillar), seat of the sun's worship.

HATHOR
Goddess depicted with a cow's head (or only cow's horns): the lady of the heavens – protectress of women, of music and of the deceased.

HEDJET
White-colored crown, symbol of rule over Upper Egypt.

HEQA (SCEPTER)
Symbol of royalty characteristic of the god Osiris.

HORUS
Divinity with a falcon's head, or depicted as a falcon; god of the sky and the pharaoh's protector. As a son of Osiris

and Isis, he is often figured as a child (Harpocrates) sucking his finger.

IBIS
Holy bird of the god Thoth, whose incarnation it was believed to be in the Late Period.

IMENTIT
Goddess of the Occident who welcomes the dead.

ISIS
Goddess, wife and sister of Osiris, mother of Horus. On her head is depicted a throne, transcribing her name.

JUSTIFIED
The epithet "justified" (*makheru*) is attributed to the dead who have received favorable judgment from Osiris.

KA
One of man's souls, representing the vital force. Also defined as "double", it is created at the same time as man himself, but is immortal and ensures him the strength needed for extraterrestrial life.

KHEPER OR KHEPRI
Divinity representing the rising sun, figured in the shape of a scarab beetle.

KHEPERESH
Blue-colored ceremonial crown with circular disks, used by the pharaoh.

KHONSU
Moon god in the shape of a boy; at Thebes he was considered a son of Amun and Mut. He is often figured with a falcon's head, adorned with a crescent moon surmounted by a lunar disk.

MAAT
Goddess of truth and justice, she is the representation of the cosmic order. Her symbol is the ostrich plume.

MERETSEGER
Female deity, often represented in the shape of a woman-headed cobra and has been identified with the Theban Peak.

MIN
Mummy-shaped god, depicted with erect phallus, his raised right arm holding a scourge, and a headdress adorned with two plumes. He was considered a protector of fertility and of the eastern desert's tracks; the seats of his worship were at Coptos and at Akhmim.

MUMMY
Desiccated dead body of the deceased wrapped up in tight bandages of fabric. The word derives from the Arabic *mumiyah*, meaning bitumen, though bitumen is found in the Egyptian mummies only in the Roman period.

MUT
Goddess originally depicted as a vulture, later represented in human shape. Amun's wife, her worship took place at Thebes.

NAOS
Stone or wooden tabernacle where the god's statue was kept, inside the shrine.

NEBRIDE
Animal skin attached to a stick, it was one of the symbols of Osiris and Anubis.

NEITH
Goddess originating from Sais in the Delta, linked to war and also to hunting; she had a protective function and, as such, played a role in the funerary cult together with Isis, Nephthys and Selkis. Later on, in the New Kingdom, she was considered a creating divinity, mother of the sun. She is depicted with the red crown of Lower Egypt; sometimes she wears on her head a shield with two crossed arrows.

NEKHAKHA
Flail, symbol of authority, characteristic of Osiris.

NEKHBET
Goddess depicted as a vulture, worshipped at El-Kab and protectress of Upper Egypt.

NEMES
Woven cap used by Egypt's rulers: it covers the head and falls back on both sides of the face.

NEPHTHYS
Sister of the goddess Isis, and Seth's wife.

NOME
Word of Greek origin indicating the different administrative districts (between 38 and 42, according to the periods) of ancient Egypt. This system of administration of the country dates back all the way to the protodynastic age and reached its supreme development in the Ptolemaic era.

NUBIA
Territory extending between the first and the fourth cataract of the Nile. It is divided into Lower Nubia, located between the first and the second cataract (called Wawat by the Egyptians), and Upper Nubia, known by the name of Kush.

NUT
Personification of the celestial vault, wife of Geb, god of the earth, and sister of Shu and Tefnut. She is represented as a woman with an arched body crossed by the stars. She is often depicted, as protectress, on the royal tombs or on the covers of coffins.

OCCIDENT, OR WEST
Represents the kingdom of the dead (where the souls of the deceased go where the sun sets).

OSIRIS
Mummy-shaped divinity, Lord of the Afterlife, Isis's husband, generated his son Horus, after his own death caused by his brother Seth. He is figured with an Atef crown, scepter and scourge. Abydos is the seat of his cult.

OSTRACON
Terracotta potsherd or stone splinter used for writing on, instead of papyrus.

PSYCHOSTASY
Weighing of the soul: after death, the soul of the deceased, that is his heart, was weighed on a two-scale balance. If it turned out to be as light as a feather (symbol of truth and justice) on the other scale it was admitted into the eternal beatitude of the kingdom of Osiris; otherwise it was devoured by a monster.

PSCHENT
Double crown symbolizing the rule over Upper and Lower Egypt, formed by the white crown inserted in the red crown.

PTAH
Creator god from Memphis, husband of the lioness-goddess Sekhmet and figured as a mummy-shaped man with the *was*-sceptre. Later he superimposed himself on Sokaris, the original god from Memphis, and was worshipped in the syncretic form of Ptah-Sokaris.

PYLON
Monumental entrance of the temples, formed by two massive trapezoid towers flanking the doorway.

PYRAMIDION
Monolithic block forming the apex of a pyramid.

RE
Ancient solar divinity originally worshipped mainly at Heliopolis. Re is represented with a falcon's head surmounted by the solar disk and with a ram's head during his nightly sailing. Starting with the Fourth Dynasty, the kings of Egypt took the title "Son of Re".

RE-HARAKHTY
Sun god - Horus of the Horizon. He is represented with a falcon aspect and a solar disk and combines the characteristics of Re and of Horus.

REGISTER
Horizontal subdivision of the decoration of the walls of tombs and temples and of objects such as the funerary stelae.

SEKHMET
Feminine divinity, represented with the head of a lioness, sometimes surmounted by a solar disk; protectress of pharaoh's royal power.

SELKIS
Goddess exercising a protective function in the funerary cult. A scorpion transcribing her name is depicted on her head.

SETH
God of chaotic forces, brother and murderer of Osiris, depicted with a human body and an unidentifiable animal's head (greyhound? ant-eater?).

SHAWABTI
Small statues working in the fields instead of the deceased in Underworld. The name derives from the verb *shwbty* (to respond), since they daily answered the call to work.

SHU
Male divinity, embodiment of the dry air, Tefnut's husband.

SISTRUM
Musical instrument (a kind of rattle) sacred to the goddess Hathor. It can either be a box in the shape of *naos* with the rattle inside, or with small, transversal metallic handle-bars.

SOLAR BOAT
Boat on which the sun-god sailed in the sky: by day he moves from east to west and by night from west to east. During his night sail (*mesektet*) the divinity was represented with a ram's head.

SONS OF HORUS
Four mummy-shaped tutelary spirits – respectively with heads of a human

being (Imset), a baboon (Hapy), a jackal (Duamutef) and a falcon (Qebhsenuef) – who protect the viscera of the deceased, contained in the four canopic jars placed in the tomb.

STELE
Slab of stone or wood, of various shapes bearing decorations and inscriptions having funerary. Of great importance are the historic stelae erected by the pharaoh for informative or propaganda purposes (large "royal stelae" or boundary stelae).

SYCAMORE
Tree sacred to the goddesses Hathor and Nut. Its very hard wood was used for the manufacture of sarcophagi and funerary accessories.

THEBAN PEAK
One of the designations of Mount El-Qurn, with its characteristic pyramidal shape, overlooking the Theban necropolises.

THOTH
Divinity depicted as ibis, or with a human body and an ibis's head, or also represented as a baboon. As inventor of writing and of sciences, he was protector of the scribes; the seat of his worship was at Hermopolis.

TOWER
See Pylon

TUTELARY SPIRIT
Demon – often mummy-shaped – which could be kindly or harmful.

UDJAT
The eye of the celestial falcon-god Horus; used as a protecting amulet.

URAEUS
Royal cobra, symbol of the light and of royalty, found on the forehead of the greater part of the divinities and of the pharaohs, in the act of rising. It was sacred to the goddess Wadjet and to the sun-god, whose eye it was believed to be.

VIZIER
Title by which the head of the executive power is indicated in ancient Egypt; he replaced the pharaoh in all the aspects of the country's administration.

WADJET
Goddess depicted as an *uraeus*, worshipped at Buto in the Delta and protectress of Lower Egypt.

WAS
Scepter characteristic of male divinities

BIBLIOGRAPHY

Baines, J., and Malek, J., *Atlas of Ancient Egypt*, Oxford and New York, 1980.

Belzoni, G. B., *Viaggi in Egitto e in Nubia*, ed. A. Siliotti, Florence, 1988.

Carter, H., and Mace, A. C., *The Tomb of Tut.Ank.Amen*, London, 1922-33.

Cenival, J. L. de, *Architecture universelle: Egypte, époque pharaonique*, Fribourg, 1964.

Curto, S., *L'Antico Egitto*, Turin, 1981.

Donadoni, S., *La civiltà egiziana*, Milan, 1940.

Farina, G., *La pittura egiziana*, Milan, 1929.

Gardiner, A. H., *Egypt of the Pharaohs*, Oxford 1974.

Goyon, J. C., *Rituels funéraires de l'ancienne Égypte*, 1972.

Grimal, N., *Histoire de l'Égypte ancienne*, Paris, 1988.

Kitchen, K.A., *Pharaoh Triumphant - The Life and Times of Ramesses II*, Warminster, 1982.

Leclant, J., et al., *Le Monde Egyptien - les pharaons*, 3 vols., Paris, 1980.

Mekhitarian, A., *La Peinture egyptienne*, Geneva, 1954.

Montet, P., *Géographie de l'Egypte ancienne*, 2 Vols., Paris, 1957-61.

Posener, G., Sauneron, S., and Yoyotte, J., *Dictionnaire de la civilisation égyptienne*, Paris, 1959.

Reeves, N., *The Complete Tutankhamun*, London 1990.

Schiaparelli, E., *Relazione dei lavori della Missione archeologica italiana in Egitto*: I, *la tomba intatta dell'architetto Kha*; II, *L'esplorazione della Valle delle Regine*, Turin, 1922-27.

Siliotti, A. (ed.), *Padova e l'egitto*, Florence, 1987.

Siliotti, A. (ed.), *Viaggiatori Veneti alla scoperta dell'Egitto*, Venice, 1985.

Siliotti, A., *Egitto - Uomini, templi e dei*, Vercelli, 1994.

Vandier, J., *Manuel d'archéologie égyptienne*, Paris, 1952-8.

THEBES

AA.VV., *Reconstitution du caveau de Sennefer dit "Tombe aux Vignes"*, Paris, 1985.

Aufrere, S., Golvin, J. C., and Goyon, J. C., *L'Egypte restituée*, Paris, 1991.

Barguet, P., *Le Temple d'Amon-Rê à Karnak. Essai d'exégèse*, Cairo, 1962.

Bruyère, B., *Rapport sur les fouilles de Deir el Médineh*, Cairo, 1924-53.

Cerny, J., *A Community of Workmen at Thebes in the Rameside Period*, Cairo, 1973.

Cerny, J, *The Valley of the Kings*, Cairo, 1973.

Golvin, J. C., and Goyon, J. C., *Les Bâtisseurs de Karnak*, Paris, 1988.

Hornung, E., *Tal der Könige*, Zurich/Munich, 1982.

Leblanc, C., *Ta Set Neferou*, Cairo, 1989.

Murnane, W. J., *United with Eternity - A Concise Guide to the Monuments of Medinet Habu*, Chicago and Cairo, 1980.

Naville, E., *The Temples of Deir el Bahari*, 4 vols., London, 1894-1908.

Porter, B., and Moss, R. L. B., *Topographical Bibliography of Ancient Egyptian Hieroglyphic Texts, Reliefs and Paintings* I, Oxford, 1960.

Reeves, N., *Valley of the Kings*, London, 1990.

Shedid, A. G., and Seidel, M., *Das Grab des Nachts*, Mainz am Rhein, 1991.

Siliotti, A., and Leblanc, C., *La Tomba di Nefertari e la Valle delle Regine*, Florence, 1993.

Steindorff, G., and Wolf, W., *Die Thebanische Gräberwelt*, Hamburg, 1936.

Werbrouck, M., *Le Temple d'Hatshepsout à Deir el Bahari*, Brussels, 1948.

Wilkinson, C. K., and Hill, M., *Egyptian Wall Paintings*, New York, 1983.

Wreszinski, W., *Atlas zur altägyptischen Kulturgeschichte*, 1915.

KEY

KV = Valley of the Kings
WV = Western Valley

QV = Valley of the Queens
TT = Theban Tombs

ILLUSTRATION CREDITS

168 *The picture shows one of the superb paintings in the tomb of Inerkhau (TT 359) in the necropolis of the workers' village of Deir el-Medina. The village provided accommodation for the artists that worked on the tombs in the Theban necropolis. Inerkhau, who lived during the eras of Ramses III and Ramses IV, had the title of "Foreman of the Lord of the Two Lands in the Seat of Truth". Here the deceased is shown adoring the grey heron, the bird considered to be the incarnation of the soul of the sun god, Ra.*

Cover
left:
Tomb of Tutankhamon, detail of the gold throne showing the portrait of Tutankhamon himself. *Photograph by Araldo De Luca/ Archivio White Star*

top right:
Tomb of Nefertari, west wall of the first annexe on the east side: the ram-headed deity between Isis and Nefti. *Photograph by Archivio Image Service*

bottom right:
Tomb of Sennegem, west wall: Sennegem and his consort adore the gods of the afterlife. *Photograph by Archivio Image Service*

Back cover, top
Tomb of Nefertari, west side. *Photograph by Alberto Siliotti*

Back cover, bottom
Golden breast-plate in the form of a falcon found in the tomb of Tutankhamon. *Photograph by Araldo De Luca*